A
MORMON CHAPLAIN

Earl S. Beecher, Ph.D., CLU, CFA

 www.trafford.com

North America & international
toll-free: 1 888 232 4444 (USA & Canada)
fax: 812 355 4082

Table of Contents

Section I.

Before Active Duty

Chapter 1.

Becoming Commissioned
as a Chaplain

In December 1949 I'd been called by the Prophet of the Church of Jesus Christ of Latter-day Saints, George Albert Smith, to serve two-years in the Central Atlantic States Mission in Virginia and North Carolina. When that time ended, my Mission President, J. Robert Price, the President of a life insurance company from Phoenix, Arizona, asked me to remain for an indefinite extended period. I was happy to do so. I was stationed in Jacksonville, North Carolina where I was serving as the Supervising Elder of the North Carolina East District. The district consisted of 14 Elders.

Ordinarily a Mission President serves about six years. After approximately three months into my extended stay, President Price had fulfilled his term and been replaced by a new man, President Martin Nalder, an undertaker from San Francisco, California who had served there as a Bishop for over 24 years. George Albert Smith had passed away and David O. MacKay had been called to be the new Prophet and President of the Church. President MacKay phoned President Nalder at the Mission Headquarters in Roanoke Virginia, and asked, "Where's Elder Beecher?"

My phone rang. President Nalder said the new Prophet had personally called and asked about me. The Draft Board in Salt Lake City had ordered me to report for pre-induction into the army on March 10, 1952. It was March 7th when I received his call. He put my release in the mail that day. I received it at noon the next day. My parents had purchased a new blue Plymouth for me to use in my mission field the year before. I began driving home immediately.

It's a long way from Jacksonville, North Carolina to Salt Lake City, Utah. I felt remorse at leaving the mission field. It had been wonderful to be able to spend full time doing the work of the Lord. I'd grown to love it there. And I was leaving behind many friends whom I was sure I'd never see again. At the same time the prospects of going home and getting on with my life were exciting.

I did not look forward to going into the army. I had served in the Utah State Guard band a couple of years and earned the rank of Sergeant. Occasionally it had involved spending time in the barracks on one of the nearby military bases. I was not fond of the regimentation of military life.

As I drove I had time to think. Ed Fernley, my close friend from college, was stationed at Fort McClelland near Montgomery, Alabama. It wasn't far out of my way. Why not stop and see him for at least a couple of hours?

Ed was within four months of completing his hitch in the service. It was good to see him. During the course of our visit he asked, "Have you ever thought about becoming a Chaplain?" I had never heard of such a possibility, much less thought about it. Ed continued, "I'd check at church headquarters and find out about it if I were you. Officers have it quite differently from enlisted men . . . no K.P., latrine duty, stuff like that."

The requirements for becoming a chaplain are different for Latter-day Saints than for Jewish, Protestant and Catholic ministers. The requirement for members of the other religious groups was a completed degree from a recognized Seminary. LDS chaplains needed to have completed a college degree in any field plus filled a full-time mission for the church.

He suggested, "You completed your Bachelors degree in Business Administration at the University of Utah before you were called on your mission, so you have the necessary academic and church qualifications. Why don't you apply for it?"

As I resumed driving I thought, besides all the things he had mentioned, it offered the opportunity to continue my missionary efforts. For strong personal reasons known only to the Lord and myself that was something I wanted very much to do.

The Draft Board had sent orders to my parents' address for me to report to Fort Douglas in Salt Lake City at 10:00 a.m. on March 10th to take physical and mental examinations as the initial step to being drafted.

It was very late in the evening of March 8th when I reached Amarillo, Texas. Next morning I ate breakfast at a local restaurant and began the final leg of my trip home at about 9:00 a.m.

It was not an easy drive. West Texas has many stretches of open, boring road. One of the service stations I stopped at to get gas had failed to close the hood of my car securely and it blew back when I was traveling at about 60 miles per hour. Suddenly there was a loud BANG! and I couldn't see anything in front except the blue of the hood blocking my view. That is exciting! I had to go back about five miles and get the station attendant to wire it shut. It was badly bent. After that I drove warily in fear it might come loose and blow open again.

I arrived in Moab, Utah at 1:00 a.m. It's located in the desolate four corners area where Colorado, New Mexico, Arizona and Utah come together. The town closes early. I could not find a room. I decided to continue driving through the night. I was lucky to find a service station manager kind enough to get out of bed and sell me some gasoline..

I arrived at Salt Lake City at 7:00 a.m. March 10th. My parents were surprised and delighted to see me. I'd been driving for 22 hours. A major storm had threatened all the way. After our greetings I said "I'm going to Fort Douglas for my exams at 10:00 a.m., but I sure feel tired."

My folks said they'd contacted the Draft Board and explained that I was still in the mission field. The Draft Board had extended my deadline two weeks. I'd driven all that way under emotional pressure without needing to. I went to bed. When I awoke I had a cold and a sore throat.

A big snowstorm had settled in. It turned out to be a good thing that I'd made the effort to arrive by March 10th after all. If I hadn't driven all night, I probably would not have been able to get through on the highways for almost two weeks.

I called Marguerite, my fiancée, and arranged a date. During my mission we had had an understanding that we would get married some day, meanwhile she should continue dating while I was away.

I found it uncomfortable getting over the strict rules of the mission field about contact of any kind with members of the opposite sex and resuming normal social patterns of behavior. Our date was not a success. At the conclusion of the evening she informed me that she'd waited while I served the 24 months. She'd waited while I remained in the field for the undetermined extra period of time my mission president had requested. She'd fulfilled any obligation she felt she owed me and she was "now free to marry Hal. Goodbye." I was devastated.

I called her the next morning and pled with her not to commit to anything with anyone else until we'd had more time to talk. We dated several times in the next few weeks. I'm happy to report that everything went well, but not smoothly. We got engaged one night. She returned my fraternity pin the next. We got engaged again the next night. She returned it again. It was an on-again off-again situation.

In the meantime my Father came down with a bad cold. He taught Civics classes at Granite High School in south Salt Lake City. The School District asked if I would be interested in substitute-teaching his classes. After all, he had all the materials ready for the classes, and so forth. He could direct me. I'd taught

Sunday School classes, and dancing lessons for Arthur Murray while I was attending the University of Utah, but I had not taught in a formal classroom situation. I decided to try it.

It was a major learning experience. One of the first things I learned was that the kids thought they were really putting over some fantastic, original pranks when they tried all the same dumb old tricks we did when I was a student. It didn't take long before they learned I was way ahead of them.

Meanwhile I decided that it would be to my benefit to be strict. I gave them a chapter to read every night. I required a written paper to be turned in every day and also gave a quiz every day. I had to read and grade all those things every evening. I was doing the work for about 45 students in each of six classes. That wasn't such a smart idea when you consider the workload, but I was desperate to do a good job.

On the last day of the week one of the young ladies from the fourth period class came up to me and said "I can't believe you're a returned missionary. They couldn't be that mean!" Up to that moment I'd not considered myself "mean" . . . just "conscientious." I guess it all depends on your point of view.

After my father returned to school the following Monday, he came home and reported he'd received a standing ovation in every class. "I hadn't realized how popular I was." I complimented him on his popularity and quietly retired to my room.

In the meantime I wrote a letter of inquiry to the Chaplains' Corps Headquarters in Washington DC to find out if my qualifications were acceptable. The reply came a couple of days before I had to report to Fort Douglas. The general tone of their letter was positive.

The day I reported to the Fort was a long one. There were more than a hundred young men in the group. They gave us physical examinations, I.Q. tests, logic tests, and so forth. At the conclusion I asked if duplicate copies of the results of all my tests could be sent to the Chaplains' Headquarters in Washington D.C. The Sergeant in charge told me it would be no problem.

I spent the next couple of weeks anxiously wondering if I could receive a commission or not. Meanwhile, my teaching experience had pleased somebody in the School District office. Almost every morning I would receive a phone call that went like this, "Mr. Jones, who teaches math at Irving Junior High School, is sick today. Can you be there by 9:00 a.m. and take over his classes?" Over the next six weeks I was called upon to teach almost every subject imaginable, English, Civics, Math, History, Music, Art, etc.

One of the more memorable experiences was when I taught the Band at South High. There was a major citywide musical event taking place. Only a portion of the band was invited to attend. I was left with about two-thirds of the band members, and they were unhappy about being left behind. Naturally I didn't know one student from another, nor did I know which instrument each one played. It was the worst sounding band I'd ever heard. I wondered how the teacher could keep his job and have a band that sounded that bad.

About ten minutes before the final bell the teacher and the rest of the band members returned. He took one horrified look and said "Clarence, what are you doing on the drums, get back to your clarinet. Alice, go back to the trumpet section where you belong. George, where's your Sousaphone? What are you doing with Clarence's clarinet?" I realized I'd been had. I determined if I ever had to teach a musical group again I'd insist on having a complete roll sheet in advance that listed the name and instrument of every class member.

Probably my worst experience occurred at the Roosevelt Junior High School. The Glee Club instructor was ill. I was expected to teach her classes the songs for an upcoming program, plus review material that had proved to be too difficult for them in the past, plus conduct the music. That wasn't so bad, but the regular accompanist was also sick, so I was trying to conduct, maintain order, and accompany on the piano while sight reading the music. Of course, that happened to be the day the School Board members made their annual visit. I wondered if the regular teacher and the accompanist hadn't become ill on that particular day as a matter of convenience.

I learned there was an LDS Servicemen's Committee that coordinated everything to do with the Military. It consisted of two Apostles and one of the Seven Presidents of Seventy, namely Harold B. Lee, Henry D. Moyle and Bruce McConkie. I phoned church Headquarters to set an appointment to obtain their endorsement regarding my qualifications to serve as an LDS Chaplain. When I arrived formal interviews were held and forms filled out. About twenty other young men were there for the same purpose. My chances looked slim.

I filled out all the forms, had them signed by the necessary General Authorities, and air mailed them Special Delivery to the Chaplains' Headquarters in Washington DC.

The LDS Servicemen's Committee was helpful in completing the information. Brother Bruce McConkie in particular had the responsibility for counseling the candidates for Chaplain. He explained that there was a Church Representative in Washington DC who met regularly with the personnel at the Chaplains' Headquarters to verify the information about each candidate and clarify his acceptance by the authorities as being qualified to represent the church in the military. Fortunately that Brother was going to be in Washington that very week, at a time convenient for considering my application.

On April 28th a letter arrived from the Chaplains' Headquarters. It explained that I had not properly completed some of the forms in triplicate. I had not had certain pages signed by a notary public. I had not filled in the word "None" in all the necessary blanks.

I spent most of that day reviewing the forms. I filled all the necessary "None" spaces and prepared the application forms as completely as I could. Then I went to Church headquarters. One of the Brethren signed as Notary Public in the right places. I airmailed the forms special delivery back to the Chaplains' Headquarters that same day.

Four days later, May 2nd to be precise, I was mowing the lawn in front of my parents' house when the telegram arrived. It was from the Chaplains' Headquarters assigning my Commission as a First Lieutenant in the United States Army, and directing me to report to The Chaplains' School at Fort Slocum, New York on May 12th for training. I grabbed that telegram and headed for Church Headquarters at 47 East South Temple Street in order to be set apart as a Chaplain and a Missionary!

Once at Bruce McConkie's office, I waited about fifteen minutes in his ante-room until he finished interviewing another candidate. Finally he came out and shook my hand.

I'm here to be set apart as a Chaplain." He looked surprised.

"Weren't you here just last week, Brother Beecher?"

"Yes."

In his uniquely patient, slow speaking way Brother McConkie began to explain the situation to me. "You realize, this is an Army position, not a Church position. We have no control over how long it takes the army to respond once you have been accepted by the Church as a suitable candidate."

As he continued his explanation I laid the telegram on his desk in front of him. He began reading it but not paying close attention as he continued his lecture. Something caught his eye. He stopped talking, paused, reread the telegram, looked up at me and said, "What did you tell those people?"

"I told them I was going to be drafted on May 20th. Unless they acted promptly they would have to go through a lot of red tape to get me released from being an enlisted man in order to commission me as a Chaplain."

He shook his head. "We've never had a commission go through in less than eighteen months from the time we gave our approval. You're telling me yours' went through in four days?" I pointed to the telegram.

"Remarkable!" He indicated we should go up to Brother Harold B. Lee's office on the next floor. It was almost like a skit being replayed the second time. Brother Lee was aware I'd been in the Church offices the week before. He began almost word for word giving both Brother McConkie and me the same explanation that Brother McConkie had just given me.

"It is an Army position, not a Church position. You must realize, Brother Beecher, that we have no control over how long it's going to take for the Chaplaincy to respond to your application." In almost exactly the same manner that I'd laid the telegram in front of Brother McConkie and pointed to it to catch his attention, Brother McConkie laid it on Brother Lee's desk and pointed to it. Brother Lee continued explaining as he read the message. Then he paused, reread it, looked up at me and said, "What did you tell those people?"

I gave him the same explanation I'd given Brother McConkie. Brother Lee repeated that the Church had never had an application approved in less than eighteen months after the candidate had received the necessary approval by the authorities. He was amazed mine had cleared in only four days. Brother McConkie and I exchanged glances. We both were enjoying the deja vue of Brother Lee's explanation and his surprise which so closely resembled Brother McConkie's own.

The next thing that occurred was one of the most remarkable experiences any young man could ask for. The third member of the L.D.S. Servicemen's Committee joined us. He was Henry D. Moyle, another member of the Quorum of the Twelve Apostles. The three of them placed their hands on my head and set me apart as a Seventy, Missionary, and Chaplain. Brother McConkie pronounced the blessing.

He blessed me with health, wisdom, the ability to concentrate, and many other choice blessings from the Lord. One thing that stood out clearly in my memory was the following phrase: "You need have no fear of physical danger, from accident, disease or enemy action. The Lord will be with you and protect you in all circumstances."

I thought to myself, "what a remarkable blessing to give a young man who's likely to be entering the field of combat in an active shooting war." It proved to be a source of security and inspiration to me throughout my entire military career.

The next few days while I was getting ready to leave for Fort Slocum I spent as much time as I possibly could with Marguerite. We made plans to get married in June just as soon as I arrived home from the six-week Basic Chaplain course.

Section II.

Active Duty within the Continental United States

Chapter 2.

The Chaplain School, Fort Slocum, New York

My orders read, "Report to the Chaplain School at Fort Slocum, New York for six weeks training beginning May 12th." Now I had to travel clear across the continent again. This time I went by train. It took four days.

I arrived at the Pennsylvania Station in New York City on a track four levels below street level. It was scary to see how the construction placed several heavy trains above each other. As I rode the escalators to the surface I thought "I hope there isn't an earthquake while I'm down here."

It was mid-afternoon when I reached the street level inside the Pennsylvania Station. The building was huge. There were hundreds, maybe thousands of people rushing about. I stepped out onto the street and stood admiring the skyscrapers. New York is indeed impressive! One of the things I liked was all the hustle and bustle. Everything moved at a rapid pace. The people seemed friendly and outgoing. They immediately spotted me as a tourist and were willing to answer my questions.

With my two suitcases in hand I found my way back down to where I caught the Shuttle. After the short trip I came to Times

Square. When I emerged at the street level I had to take a few moments to admire it. I had often seen it in movies. Here I was, standing in the real thing.

After wandering around for a while and doing a little shopping at the usual tourist traps I went down a couple of levels to find the correct subway train. As memory serves it was the "AA" train. I learned "AA" stood for an express. "A" stood for a slower, local train that went to the same locations throughout the city as the "AA" train did. I had often heard Duke Ellington's record of "Take The 'A' Train", but I had never understood what it meant, although the lyrics were pretty clear that it was the way to get to Harlem, whatever that was. Now the words took on meaning. Harlem is an area in New York located in upper Manhattan. Upper means where the streets have higher numbers and lower means where the streets have smaller numbers. "Uptown" and "Downtown" are related to the street number designations. Simple, once you learn it.

Catching a subway train in New York is a unique experience. The stations are underground, dirty, and crowded. People rush here and there to catch trains, arrive on trains, and depart for the surface above. The trains pull rapidly into the station, load, and move out quickly. You have to hasten to get on board before the doors close. Meanwhile other people rush to get ahead of you unless you assert yourself.

Somehow I held on to my two suitcases, pushed into the crowd of people who were surging ahead of me, and caught the correct train. As I sat by the window, tunnels with huge supporting pillars, then tenements, then more tunnels and pillars raced by as I rode it to the end of the line. There I caught a train to New Rochelle. I was impressed by the speed of the subway as it traveled underground, then on elevated areas past many buildings, and then across the open countryside. The whole trip from Times Square to New Rochelle took about forty-five minutes. My thoughts were confused and apprehensive. It wasn't as if I'd never been away from home before, but this was a time of change, of insecurity and doubt.

The conductor called "New Rochelle." I broke away from my musing and faced reality. I rearranged my tie and jacket, gathered my suitcases and stepped off the train into the small depot. A short cab ride and I was at the ferry dock, waiting to go to David's Island in Long Island Sound. The Chaplain School occupied the entire island.

After about half an hour the ferry arrived and I walked aboard. The weather was clear and beautiful. The temperature was ideal. The ferry was a small boat that only took about five minutes to cross Long Island Sound to David's Island. The sun was setting. It brought to mind the ferry boat trips I'd taken in San Francisco harbor when I was a child. I'd liked standing on the bottom level and looking at the water close by. This was similar, but the boat was so much smaller that there was no upper level. I had to stand at the water's edge. The ride was smooth and invigorating. The ferryman told me "the School Headquarters are in that direction." So there I headed.

David's Island was truly beautiful. It was like a circle about two or three city blocks in diameter. In the center was a huge green lawn the size of two or three football fields that made up the parade ground. Around the edges were red brick buildings. Some were large office buildings; others were private dwellings.

I must have made an unusual picture at 6'2" tall, weighing 128 pounds, dressed in my black "preaching suit," white shirt, black tie, and carrying two large heavy mis-matched suitcases.

I walked from the landing toward the larger buildings. It was twilight. The lights on the lampposts came on and added to the charm of the place. It was peaceful, one of the most quiet and beautiful moments I can recall. What a contrast to New York City, only forty five minutes away. I walked along a street that was behind the private dwellings that faced the Parade Ground. One red brick building stood out. It was the largest on the Island. It was a little more than two blocks from the ferry landing. I hoped it would be the Administration Building that was the headquarters of The Chaplain School. When I came around to the front, the

Parade Ground side, there was a sign that said it was the Post Headquarters.

I was so tired I literally dragged my heavy suitcases up the front steps. As I entered the building my first impression was that it was empty. There was a long hall. At the far end I saw an office with some lights. Then I became aware that a radio was playing softly, so someone was there. I felt awkward reporting in. I did not know if I should salute or not, especially since I was in civilian clothes. I was relieved when the man on duty was a Corporal. I knew I need only salute officers. Whew! The first hurdle was cleared.

The Corporal informed me the Chaplain School Headquarters was separate from the Post Headquarters. "It's two blocks that way." I thanked him, hoisted up my suitcases and headed for the new destination.

Upon arriving at the Chaplain School Headquarters I was confronted by another man on duty at a desk. This time it was a Warrant Officer. I elected to salute him. He smiled, and pleasantly informed me "it is not necessary to salute when you are in 'civies'." He had me sign in, accepted a copy of my orders and directed me to follow him. I picked up my suitcases and huffed and puffed the two blocks to my new quarters. He set a rapid pace.

Upon arrival we climbed the three stories to the top floor of the building. He quickly introduced me to three fine looking young men my same age, and left. There were four bunks in the room. They indicated I could have the fourth one . . . on top, farthest away from the window.

I unpacked my suitcases into the chest of drawers. Then one of the fellows walked me to the basement of the building where I checked out a mattress cover, sheets, pillow cases and blankets. I was exhausted. It felt good to stretch out on a cot that didn't vibrate and swing with every rotation of railroad wheels.

Just as I was getting settled and breathing easy, there was the sound of footsteps rushing up the stairs. One of the largest men I had ever seen burst into the room. He was a Sergeant. "Are you Beecher?" he demanded.

"Yes, sir" I replied. He surely did not look like a man to argue with. He had a Corporal and two Privates with him.

"Are you a Chaplain or a Chaplain's Assistant?"

"A Chaplain."

"Oh, you're in the wrong building!"

With that, he began ordering people in a flurry of activity that left me breathless. They took all my belongings out of the drawers, repacked them into my suitcases, rolled up my bedding and moved me to the adjacent building. For a moment I half expected him to throw me over his shoulder and carry me too! Fortunately, he didn't.

It seemed like I was settled in a matter of seconds. My new room was on the ground floor at the front of the building with a window that overlooked the parade ground. My bed had been expertly made. My belongings were unpacked and arranged neatly in the drawers. The Sergeant surveyed the results, satisfied. "Sir, would you come with me to headquarters, please?"

That was the first time in my army career I was addressed as "Sir."

"Is there a problem?"

"I'm not sure, sir. I was instructed to bring you back to the officer on duty."

We walked even faster on the return than we had walked going over, only this time I wasn't struggling to carry any suitcases.

On reporting in, the Warrant Officer informed me that my orders read for me to report to the Chaplain School on May 12th, and that I had followed them precisely. However, that was the day the course for Chaplains' Assistants began. Since I looked about the age of most of the Assistants, he had assumed I belonged in that class. The Chaplains' course didn't begin until May 19th. I was a week early.

"Do you know anyone in New York you could visit for a week?"

"One of my married college chums lives there." I'd intended to look him up at the earliest opportunity. The Warrant Officer suggested that I "go visit him and come back in a week." That week as a civilian in New York City was the beginning of my active duty army career.

As I headed back to my room the air was growing cool. The evening was impressively beautiful. The lawn was almost iridescent and several acres across. The large buildings stood in silhouette against the moonlight sky. The moon was barely rising above the horizon. As I walked it would disappear, reappear, then disappear behind one building after another.

I remember lying on my cot that night, listening to the earphones of a tiny missile-shaped radio I'd bought that afternoon at a tourist shop in the city. I looked out at the moonlight on the parade grounds. I had a feeling of peace at last, after the hectic four-day trip on the train, subway, the train etc. I thanked my Heavenly Father that I'd arrived safely. I thanked Him again for this new opportunity to serve Him. I had a good feeling about this new adventure in my life.

When I awoke the next morning I went to the mess hall for breakfast. It was served on metal trays from steam tables. The food was good. Best of all, there was plenty of it. I felt self-conscious because I was the only one there in civilian clothes. Everyone else was in uniform. Some of the young men from the barracks that I had seen the night before greeted me, but nobody sat by me. I ate alone.

I went to the Administration Building. There was a different officer on duty. I asked him questions about how I should go about getting uniforms, where I should be, and when, etc. He told me that there was nothing for me to do until the 19th. He also recommended I spend the week in New York City with friends, "but be back on the evening of the 18th so you're ready for class early the morning of the 19th." He said they would check into my uniform allowance, and as soon as it was approved I could buy them at the Commissary. Officers buy their own uniforms with an allowance that is given to them in cash.

I thanked him and set out for New York. The walk to the ferry dock was brisk. David's Island is lovely on a spring morning. The ferry ride was fun. The railway station in New Rochelle is small.

It was late enough in the day that most of the daily commuters had already gone to work so it wasn't crowded. The Attendant took time to be helpful. He gave me a map of New York City and information about how the trains connect to the subway.

I enjoyed seeing the countryside and the big city. The buildings loomed high on every side. There were dirty backyards with clothes hanging on the clotheslines and children playing. Once in a while I could see into the open doors of warehouses as we flashed past them doing about seventy miles an hour. There was hustle and bustle inside each of them. Then the subway went underground. Huge supporting pillars zoomed closely past the train's darkened windows. It was still magic.

Despite it being a work day I tried calling my friend, Dick Neff's, number. No one was home. That was no surprise. I decided to do some leisurely shopping. I've always been a collector of big band records. Four years earlier, in 1948, my parents and I had taken an automobile trip around the United States which included being in New York City. I knew that many wonderful record-collector stores were on Sixth Avenue so I headed there. I spent most of the day just wandering around. I ate at the Automat. I reserved a room at the YMCA. I'd heard it was the cheapest lodgings available, and I didn't have much money to spend.

Finally I managed to reach Dick. He was working so he couldn't spend time with me. "I plan to take next Tuesday off so we can spend the day together." He then told me of many exciting things to do and see in New York. I was pretty much on my own. I remember going to the Statue of Liberty. It was a wonderful ferry ride from Manhattan to Bedloes Island. I climbed all the way to the top of the staircase inside the Statue so I could look at the skyline of Manhattan out of the windows in her crown.

I visited several art museums. I saw original paintings by many artists I'd admired. I wasn't impressed by a display at the Museum of Modern Art. Room after room was filled with what looked like huge background washes in semi-oval shape. These were not pictures, just pastel colored washes which resembled giant individual frames from a movie film. I thought, "Why is anyone excited over these? They surely don't compare to Rembrandt or Van Gogh! Oh well, I guess one must get with the times and admire whatever someone else says is 'in'," but I couldn't convince myself to do so.

Sunday morning I attended the Manhattan Ward on 81st Street. Almost everyone in the whole Church attends that Ward at one time or another. It was like "Old Home Week." I saw childhood friends, classmates from high school and the University of Utah. One of my friends from the Lambda Delta Sigma fraternity at the University was serving in the bishopric. Even a couple of my former missionary companions were there that weekend.

During the Gospel Doctrine class, the instructor said, "If you feel this ward is not friendly because the person next to you has not extended his hand and made you welcome, there's an understandable reason. Will everyone who is visiting today please stand?" Over eighty percent of the people in the class stood up, including everyone on the row I was sitting on. We all laughed. It broke the ice. Soon everyone had greeted everyone else and the lesson began.

Dick and his wife Pat were in attendance. We arranged to see each other the next Tuesday, the day before I was to report back to Fort Slocum. Dick took the day off as he'd promised. We decided to go to Jones Beach.

We arrived at the beach at about 9:30 that morning and stayed until 4:00 p.m. The sand at Jones Beach is white. It's very pretty and reflects the sunlight in a pleasing manner. We were in and out of the water all day. Pat had prepared a picnic lunch that we munched on continually. It was one of the most pleasant days I can recall. Since it was an overcast day we didn't consider the possibility of getting sunburned.

They drove me back to Times Square. I was surprised Dick drove so aggressively. All four fenders had sizable dents. I remembered him as very quiet, almost introverted. Here he hollered at other drivers and waved his fist at them. He saw the expression on my face and said "You have to learn to drive New York City style in order to survive." We all laughed about it.

By the time we reached Times Square, I was beginning to itch. When I arrived at Fort Slocum it was evening. Again I enjoyed a beautiful walk in the twilight. I reached my room and discovered my bunk had been reserved for me, and I had a roommate. He was formerly a Methodist minister from Los Angeles. He held the rank of Major. He had been on active duty a few months and this was his first opportunity to attend the Chaplain School. It was then I understood how fortunate I was to begin my army career with training in the school. Many of the men in attendance had been on active duty for several months before receiving any formal instruction as to how they were to function.

We went to the mess hall, ate dinner and got acquainted. He introduced me to several other Chaplains. It was evident that all of them had graduated from Seminary except the "Mormons." They represented all the major faiths. There were six Jewish chaplains, six Catholic chaplains, five Episcopal, six Baptist, two Christian Scientist, four or five Methodist, six Lutheran, four Presbyterian, five Mormon, and I can't recall all the rest.

I sought out the Mormon brethren. The four of them shared a room upstairs. I was not housed with the others because I'd arrived first and selected a room downstairs. They had arrived together and chosen a room together. They didn't even know I was registered until we met after dinner. There was a minor difference between my Mormon brothers and me. I had attended the University of Utah and majored in business, they had all attended the Brigham Young University. I don't know what their majors were. Two of them were older than I; two were about my age. All of them had had previous active duty experience before coming to the school.

My Methodist roommate was one of the kindest, most considerate men I'd ever met. He had deep spiritual convictions that impressed me. We held long discussions about the Bible and compared our beliefs. Through these discussions we developed a mutual respect for each other's churches.

My clothing allotment had not come through. The first couple of days in class I was the only chaplain in civilian clothes. It made me stand out. Everyone soon knew who Beecher was. I hated being different.

I'd developed a terrible sunburn. I went to the dispensary and the attendant gave me some salve. I called Dick and Pat to see how they were doing. They'd been burned so severely that their doctor ordered them to bed for a week! I was always lucky that I could tan to the point of being suspected of belonging to another race without suffering from the burn. But this one was the worst I'd ever had. Clothing itched and hurt. It was almost torture to sit in the classroom. It felt even worse when my clothing allotment finally cleared about a week later and I bought my uniforms. They were wool. I'm allergic to wool. They itched almost beyond the limits of endurance. Somehow I survived. I still remember sitting those itchy, sweaty hours in the classroom waiting for the time to pass so I could go back to my BOQ and take off those hot woolen clothes.

All in all the school was a pleasant experience once the sunburn had run its course.

I recall a couple of experiences worth relating. The six Jewish Chaplains represented the three classic viewpoints, orthodox, conservative and reform. They would hold heated "discussions" among themselves in their quarters which happened to be the room next to mine. I would eavesdrop. Finally I got nerve enough to begin to visit them and sit listening.

One afternoon Chaplain Zion said to me, "Beecher, you're all the time sitting here listening to us. What do you think about all this?"

"It's wonderful. You're giving me a better understanding of the Old Testament. I hope you don't mind my being here."

They all agreed, "We don't mind. In fact, we have a few questions we'd like to ask you. You Mormons think you're of the household of Israel and you make claims to that effect, don't you?"

"Yes. I'm of the tribe of Joseph through Ephraim."

"How can you say that? Ephraim's tribe is among the lost tribes." That's when I opened my mouth and inserted my foot. "Not anymore. I'm here."

If you haven't been grilled by six Rabbis for three hours, you haven't lived. It's an experience. Once through it you look back on it as a pleasure. At the time you're not sure how well you're presenting your beliefs.

The discussion followed along these lines. "How do you know you're from Ephraim?"

"I had a Patriarch in my church place his hands on my head and by the power of the Melchizedec Priesthood give me a Patriarchal Blessing. In the blessing he told me I was from the tribe of Ephraim. As far as Ephraim's being one of the lost tribes, you all know that in Deuteronomy 33: 17, where it describes Joseph's receiving his patriarchal blessing from Israel, his father, he was promised his tribe would be the first to be gathered in the last days, and that 'tens of thousands from Ephraim, and thousands from Manasseh' would be sent to gather the other tribes. And the last tribe to be gathered in preparation for the coming of the Messiah would be Judah's tribe"

In shock they said "You're quoting Moses to us!?"

"Why not? He was from the tribe of Levi. I have as much claim to him as you do. I'm from Ephraim. You're from Judah. He didn't belong any closer to your tribe than to mine. You have to realize, we Mormons look at the Jewish people as first cousins. We're all from the house of Israel."

They looked at each other and sort of shook their heads. "We didn't realize the Mormons felt any affinity toward the Jews."

"Of course we do. Our mission is to prepare for the coming of the Messiah. You've had the same mission for thousands of years. We have a lot in common."

The next three hours were spent discussing the mission of Joseph Smith and the establishment of the church.

On of their first questions was "why are you called Mormons?" I explained that the correct name of the church is The Church of Jesus Christ of Latter-day Saints. "

"First you need to understand that the Book of Mormon is the record of the tribe of Joseph, particularly through the hand of Ephraim. In his 37th chapter, Ezekiel prophesied that it would come forth and be joined with the record of the tribe of Judah (the Bible) before the Jews returned to the land of Israel. Isaiah prophecied that an unlearned man would bring forth a sealed book that was the record of a destroyed people in his 29th chapter. This was to happen before the forests of Lebanon were replanted."

The Book of Mormon tells the story of a group of people who belonged to Joseph's tribe who were led by a prophet named Lehi. In 600 B.C. he was warned to leave Jerusalem before the Babylonians invaded.

He took his family into the wilderness where they built a boat and sailed to a promised land. It turned out to be America. Once here his people grew to be numerous. They split into two groups called Nephites and Lamanites. They were constantly at war. The prophets among the Nephites recorded their history. At the end of about a thousand years there was a final battle in which the Nephites were destroyed. The Lamanites remained and became the forefathers of the various American groups of Indians.

Mormon was the name of one of the last prophets of the Nephites. He lived about 400 A.D. He took all the previous records and abridged them into one volume. When Joseph Smith was given the ancient record to translate, he was given Mormon's abridgement. Because the church accepts that ancient record from the American prophets as scripture, in addition to the Bible, enemies gave us the nickname "Mormons."

The Jews have suffered persecution because of their beliefs. So have the "Mormons." If you read Jeremiah 31, you will see that his prophecy clearly refers to the tribe of Ephraim (not the Jews) in the last days. The trek of the Mormon Pioneers fulfills that prophecy. The establishment of the temple in Salt Lake City fulfills Isaiah 2 and Micah 4.

Then I was asked, what is so special about temples, and who is that on top of your temples? Is it Gabriel?

The statue on the top of each of our temples is Moroni, not Gabriel, although he holds a horn. He is the "ensign to the nations" prophesied in Isaiah 16. In the last days he is to come and announce the restoration of the full gospel, including the records of the whole earth and not just the eastern half. In mortal life he was Mormon's son. Just before he died his father gave him charge of the ancient records. He wrote some final messages then buried them. Fourteen hundred years later he returned as a resurrected Angel to lead Joseph Smith to their hiding place.

"I know you don't accept the New Testament, but there is a prophecy in Revelations 14 that speaks of an Angel who will bring the full gospel to the earth just prior to the return of the Messiah. When he appeared Moroni identified himself to Joseph Smith as that Angel."

I had mentioned concerning the return of the Jews to their Holy Land and Ezekiel wrote that the ancient book dealing with the tribe of Joseph was to be brought forth before that event. In October 1842 Joseph Smith directed Orson Hyde, one of the early Apostles of our church who was of Jewish descent, to go to the Holy Land and dedicate it for the return of the Jews. In the March 1843 issue of the Millennial Star Orson Hyde published his dedicatory prayer in which he predicted that the British would take over that land, then they would turn it over to the Jews for the restoration of the nation of Israel.

General Allenby of the British Army took control of the land in 1917. The United Nations recognized the nation of Israel in 1947.

Isaiah wrote that the sealed book concerning the destroyed people would be brought forth by an unlearned man before the forests of Lebanon would be restored. The Jews have replanted the forests of Lebanon. Everything is progressing right on schedule.

We are the only church group that anticipated the restoration of Israel as a nation.

We also discussed the mission of Elijah. "You good Jewish people set a place at your table for him on certain occasions. You need to know that Elijah appeared in our first temple, at Kirtland

Ohio to restore to Joseph Smith the keys of the sealing power to seal families together for eternity in 1836.

You asked what was special about our temples, much of the work that we do in our temples deals with family history and sealing families together for eternity. That was the mission of Elijah and why he was prophesied to return. Shortly after his appearance the spirit of family history research became widespread. The Church is leading the way with the greatest genealogical research facilities available anywhere.

Even Moses himself appeared in that temple and gave Joseph Smith the keys to the "gathering of Israel." The missionary system of our church is a modern marvel in the eyes of most observers. First there were to be tens of thousands from Ephraim's tribe, followed by thousands from Manasseh's tribe. Eventually all the tribes will come forth, and finally Judah's.

At the end of our discussion we were all good friends.

Goldberg and Rabinowitz, the two Orthodox chaplains, even invited me to join them for dinner in the kosher kitchen. Up until that time I had heard of the requirements for things to be "kosher," but I'd never understood what was involved. The conservative and reform chaplains ate in the regular mess hall. They didn't observe the kosher rituals.

Another event worth remembering occurred in the Army Organization class. The instructor was a Methodist with the rank of Captain. I was a First Lieutenant, the lowest rank a Chaplain can hold. When it came to organization theory, as a business management major in school I was probably ahead of the rest of the class. They had majored in theology. We were seated in alphabetical order so I was located near the middle of the front row.

The one thing that is not taught in the Chaplain School is religion. Every chaplain in attendance is an ordained minister from his own denomination. With Jewish, Catholic, Protestant and LDS chaplains in attendance, it is obvious there is not going to be a uniformity of doctrine among them.

At the close of the hour the Methodist Captain chose to conclude the lesson with a very brief quote from the New Testament. Personally I felt it was the "garnish on the cake." It summarized and expressed the point of the lesson beautifully.

It did not sit well with the Jewish Major who was seated on my immediate right. "Don't quote that garbage in here!" he said loud and clear. The instructor was caught off guard. He probably hadn't even realized what he had done. He was a good man used to quoting scripture.

The firey Hard-Shell Baptist "bird" Colonel on my immediate left took exception to the Jewish chaplain's remark. "What do you mean 'garbage'?"

"I mean that New Testament crap!"

"I suppose you would rather he quoted the Old Testament!"

"Well, at least that's scripture."

"That's all been fulfilled and done away with except for maybe some of the Psalms and Proverbs."

"That's your opinion!"

The Baptist Colonel stood up, towering over me with his fists clenched. I was sitting between them with my head swiveling back and forth as if I were in the middle of the tennis match. I felt very uncomfortable. They weren't at that moment going to be able to settle an argument that had been going on for 2000 years. I started to laugh, partly to relieve the tension and partly because it really was kind of funny.

"Beecher, what are you laughing at?" the Colonel demanded.

"All I can say is . . . thank God for the Book of Mormon." The whole class burst into laughter. They realized that the Jewish brother was not going to accept the New Testament, even as the Catholic and Protestant brothers did not accept the Book of Mormon. The whole thing was a comparable situation. The laughter relieved the tension.

Soon everybody stood up and started to leave the room. As I arose the instructor signaled for me to lag behind. I was worried about what he might say concerning my comment and behavior in class. He sidled up beside me and said, "I may not agree with your doctrine, but thank you."

Another event that left a lasting impression occurred when we five LDS Chaplains spent a weekend together in New York City. I'd heard the old song about "the Bowery, the Bowery, I'll never go there anymore." I'd never understood the meaning behind the song. We decided to go into New York City together and attend the Manhattan Ward on Sunday. On Saturday we wound up in the Bowery.

It was one of the saddest places I've ever seen. People were passed out on the sidewalk, in the doorways. I counted 83 in one block. There were homeless people everywhere. Most of them were drunk. As we walked past one bar a "customer" came flying out. He was being physically ejected with such force that he didn't land until he was clear across the sidewalk. He almost collided with Chaplain Parr while still in mid-air.

Everywhere there were people begging for money. "A Dime, a dime. Can you spare a dime for a cup of coffee?" We knew it wasn't coffee they wanted. Chaplain Parr made the mistake of giving one particularly pitiful old man a dime. Immediately there were about 200 people following us demanding dimes. One toothless old crone came and linked her arm in his and held on to him for almost a block. He had a bad time tactfully shaking her off.

"You're all men of the cloth. Can't you help a brother out in his time of need?" The crowd was very good at working on your sense of guilt.

Chaplain Mortenson took a picture of us with the crowd. Then they really started shouting and demanding money for posing. The whole thing was embarrassing. Nevertheless, it did not embarrass the crowd. They had the routine polished to an art so they could work on any tourists who happened to come by. Chaplains proved to be special targets. It took us about three blocks of rapid walking to outdistance them.

When we were free, Chaplain Widdison turned to Chaplain Parr. "Whatever possessed you to give that guy the first dime?" He defended himself "You could all see he needed it. I felt sorry for him. I didn't realize it was going to start a near riot."

"If you were really going to help him, it would take more than a dime."

"Can you imagine what would have happened if I'd given him a dollar?"

Chaplain Parsons reacted, "I shudder to think about it."

Well, so much for the Bowery. That was many years ago. What must it be like now!

One other amusing event comes to mind. The big Sergeant was assigned to teach us how to march. I had been in marching bands most of my life, so I was familiar with the routine. However, most of the other gentlemen of the cloth had not had any such experience.

We were on the parade field. It was a very hot day. We were sweaty and uncomfortable in the open sunlight. However, we were happy to be outside, out of the classroom. We'd been marching about an hour and were tired.

The Sergeant said "Now I'm going to teach you 'Column Right.' Pay close attention. After you hear the warning word 'Column' you continue stepping forward until you hear the command 'Right!' At that point you take one more step forward on your right foot, then you plant you left foot and turn 90 degrees to the right, then step smartly to your right on your right foot. Now everyone do that as I give the command."

He gave the command. The man behind me continued forward and bumped into me from the back. The man in front of me did a complete about-face and bumped into me from the front, and the man to my left did a right turn and collided into me from the side. I never saw such confusion. It was funny. Nobody knew what to do.

The Sergeant became upset. He started to swear at us, then quickly caught himself as he realized he was addressing a group of Chaplains. He almost turned purple. I couldn't help laughing to myself. Several of the other Chaplains started laughing. The

Sergeant didn't see any humor in it. It only irritated him all the more.

He explained the whole procedure again and gave the command. Almost the same thing happened. He was really beside himself, yet he managed to refrain from using profane language. Finally in the most condescending and sarcastic manner he could muster he let us have it for being so stupid.

One of the Chaplains, who held the rank of Colonel, was irritated by the Sergeant's inclination to use bad language and address us with disrespect.

"Sergeant, if you don't like the way we execute a 'Column Right', I suggest you quit demonstrating a 'By The Right Flank' and correctly show us how to do a 'Column Right'. I also suggest you learn the difference!"

I've never seen a man so crestfallen as the Sergeant was at that moment. The Chaplain was right. The Sergeant had demonstrated it incorrectly. From that moment the Sergeant showed more respect toward all of us. Some of the older Chaplains had been around a few years and knew the army game better than the Sergeant did, and he now realized it.

The six weeks course passed rapidly. In the last week I got a phone call from Marguerite. She wanted to call off our wedding.

I caught the train home. Another four days of vibration! When I arrived at the station in Salt Lake City, there was Marguerite, her folks, my folks . . . It seemed that everybody from both families was there to meet me. Everyone looked downcast and worried. I wound up trying to cheer them up and let them know everything was all right. "Marguerite and I can work it out."

The original plan was to have the wedding within a couple of days from the time I arrived home. Marguerite even had the refreshments prepared, the invitations printed, and the envelopes addressed. At the last minute she got cold feet. She explained it this way. "I waited while you were on your two-year mission. I waited the indefinite extra time you were asked to stay out there. You were here for a few dates, then you were off to the Army. I haven't seen very much of you in the last two years and I'm not sure marrying you is the right thing to do."

I didn't have much time to discuss it with her. I was assigned to Camp Cooke in California and I had to leave within two days. We decided to postpone getting married until some later, indefinite date.

Chapter 3.

Camp Cooke, California

I decided it would be an advantage to have transportation readily available while I was on the post, so I drove my car to California. Besides I was tired of riding on trains. I began the trip from Salt Lake to Los Angeles one morning in July.

The route called for me to pass through Beaver, Utah, a small town about 200 miles south of Salt Lake City where I had lived as a boy. I decided to look up Jim Hickman, my childhood best friend.

When I got to Beaver I was told that Jim didn't live there anymore. His family had moved to Cedar City a couple of years after I moved away. It had been fourteen years since I left. However, Jim's father happened to be in town that day. He was in a store a couple of doors away from the place where I'd gone to inquire. He gave me Jim's address and phone number in Los Angeles. I thought, "That's great. It's right where I'm headed. I'll look him up there."

One of the first things I did when I arrived in L.A. was to call Jim's phone number. He wasn't home. I decided I'd better head on to Camp Cooke which was about a four hour drive away.

When I arrived at Camp, I reported to the Post Chaplain's office. Everyone greeted me warmly and said they were "happy to have me aboard." Then I reported to the headquarters of the Engineering Battalion to which I had been assigned. The Adjutant there was one of the best informed, friendly and intelligent men I've ever met. He subsequently guided me concerning army protocol or ticklish matters that arose. There were to be plenty of them.

After getting settled in my BOQ, I went to the mess hall and ate dinner. Afterward there was nothing to do so I began contacting some of the LDS personnel on the post. I soon ran into a Sergeant Smith in the MPs. He turned out to be an overgrown kid. He liked to tease and give other people a hard time. Sergeant Smith introduced me to several other LDS men, and we decided to go to the movies in the nearby town of Lompoc. The Adjutant showed me how to sign out VOCO (Vocal Order of the Commanding Officer) at my battalion headquarters.

We were all dressed in civilian clothes. I got into the Sergeant's car and we headed for the main gate. The Guard wanted to check our passes. Smith unnecessarily began giving him a hard time. The guard began to get upset and demanded to see the Sergeant's drivers license, etc. He handed him his wallet.

The Guard told him "You're an M.P. You know better than that. Take it out of your wallet like you're supposed to!" He responded "If you want to see it, take it out yourself." They got into a controversy. The situation escalated. The Guard demanded to see everyone's pass. There were six of us in the car. Each of the fellows dutifully handed him his pass. Of course, I didn't have one. I had merely signed out.

That was the last straw for the Guard. He decided we were all acting improperly. We were ordered out of the car and escorted into a building nearby. I was disgusted with Sergeant Smith at that point. Both he and the Guard had acted in an emotional, illogical, childish way. The duty Officer looked at the passes. Then he came to me. I told him simply "I signed out VOCO and don't have a pass."

"Are you an officer?" he asked.

"Yes, I'm the new Chaplain. I just arrived on the post today.

"You're a Chaplain?" he asked. "What are you doing here with these guys?"

"We all belong to the same church. We decided to go to a movie. When we got to the gate this man and the guard both began behaving like a couple of spoiled children. I wouldn't place the blame on either one. They both acted in an unprofessional manner."

The duty Officer quickly decided to dismiss the whole affair after telling everyone they should not bring trivial matters to his attention. As we walked back to the car the Guard explained he'd "had a bad day, and everything had gone wrong. I hope I haven't offended you, sir." I just told him he should use a little more patience in dealing with people, and particularly with "children like the Sergeant."

When we were back in the car and on our way, one of the men said, "If you hadn't been with us, they probably would've thrown the book at us. We could've been detained for hours."

I said simply, "I don't understand what it was all about. Smitty, why didn't you just show him your pass and act like you're expected to? What was your purpose for all the fuss?"

He didn't answer. One of the other men said, "It was lucky you outranked the Duty Officer. He wasn't going to put you in the Stockade."

That got to me. I said, "That would have been just great! The new Chaplain gets arrested his first night on the post. What news that would have made. Sergeant, don't you ever put me in an embarrassing situation like that again!"

That was my first day's introduction to my first full time active duty post.

Chapter 4.

A Lesson In Authority

The 44th Infantry Reserve Division from Illinois had been activated as a single unit and brought to Camp Cooke. The Korean War was hot. Men were being pulled out of these reserve units and sent overseas individually as the need for replacements there arose. I found myself a stranger in the midst of a tight community of friends that had been transported from one State to another.

The Post Chaplain was from California and the Division Chaplain was part of the tight-knit group from Illinois. The Division Chaplain was responsible for the Illinois people exclusively. The Post Chaplain served everyone on the post which included several other army units besides the Illinois Division. I had minimal contact with the Post Chaplain.

My assignment was to Chapel E. Geographically it was located about the center of the Camp. It served personnel from all units, but particularly the Illinois Division.

My organization assignment was to the Engineering Battalion which was part of the 44th Division. Then I was given a secondary official assignment to the Medical Battalion which was also from that same division.

I was soon to learn the difference between line and staff authority. I had studied it in school, but this was a practical lesson that drove the message home.

My line commander was the Lieutenant Colonel from the Engineering Battalion. The Adjutant explained that his orders were to take precedence over any other officer's orders except someone higher than he who could ultimately give orders to him. But anyone who understands the chain of command would not give me direct orders different from his. They would tell him what to tell me.

Another thing I learned was that Chaplains do not carry command. They may have rank, but they do not have the right to give direct orders like other commissioned officers do.

Being a Chaplain is a unique position. You are an officer, yet you are not expected to be tied down by all the rules of protocol that other officers are. Yet you are expected to follow them. In addition you are expected to act as dictated by the religious and emotional needs of the military personnel and their families. You are the minister for the troops in your unit regardless of their individual religious affiliation. For example, a Chaplain is the only commissioned officer who is not considered out of place when he enters the Enlisted Men's Service Club or the N.C.O.'s Service Club.

The Chaplain is responsible to see that Protestant services are held for the Protestant personnel, Mass for the Catholics, services for the Buddhists, Sacrament and Priesthood meetings for the Mormons, Jewish services for the Jews, etc. You don't personally conduct the Mass or services for denominations other than your own, you arrange to have a properly recognized authority from each denomination hold their respective services.

Officially the Army recognizes only four religious categories: Catholic, Protestant, Jewish, and everyone else regardless of their beliefs. For example, only a Catholic Priest holds Mass. A Jewish Rabbi conducts their services. Mormons are lumped into the Protestant category, although the LDS church is not a protestant church.

I was classified as a Protestant Chaplain and was expected to hold services appropriate for all Protestant groups to meet in a single worship service. Some of the Protestant Chaplains, such as the Episcopalians, hold very liturgical services. Others, such as the Baptists and Methodists hold services that are not liturgical in nature. The Pentecostal Chaplains have their own unique form of worship.

Over the next three years I held services jointly with Protestant Chaplains from all these groups. I gave the sermon while another chaplain led the liturgy, or vice versa. Often I did the whole service when another chaplain was not available.

My best lesson in Line and Staff authority came early in my tour. I met once a week with the 44th Division Chaplain and all the other Chaplains in that Division to coordinate our activities. That meant we would schedule services at our various chapels at hours that did not conflict with each other. This gave the men and their families the opportunity to select the time and Chapel most convenient for them to attend. It also meant that we did not have Vespers on evenings that overlapped, etc. We also scheduled our Character Guidance lectures so all the units were covered regardless of which Battalion or Company we were assigned to. There were some companies that did not have a Chaplain assigned to them full time. We covered their needs also.

One morning when the regular weekly meeting with the Division Chaplain was scheduled, my Colonel from the Engineering Battalion asked me to run an emergency errand to a nearby city. I called the Division Chaplain's office and left word that I couldn't attend the meeting, but that I would coordinate my activities for the week as soon as I got back. I performed the errand and returned to the post that afternoon.

Upon arriving back at Battalion headquarters I learned the Division Chaplain had exploded over my "failure to follow his orders." He had come to my Battalion Headquarters and began upbraiding the Adjutant in a most unbecoming manner. My Engineering Colonel arrived in time to hear part of his tirade. The Adjutant was his "right hand" and he wasn't going to permit anybody to speak to his man in that manner. The two Colonels got into a major argument. The Engineering Colonel ordered the Division Chaplain off our Battalion premises and gave him a direct order "never to get in touch with my chaplain again!"

Wow! What was I supposed to do? The adjutant tactfully filled me in on the whole situation. Despite the fact that he had been the recipient of most of the abuse, he found my situation amusing. He really was a good friend.

"Well, Chappie, what do you do now?"

"I don't know. Do you think I can get the Colonel to change his mind?"

"I doubt it. He's really steamed. There's more to this than meets the eye. You see, those two guys have known each other for years, and they don't like each other. Besides, the Colonel is Catholic and the Chaplain is Lutheran. That doesn't help matters much either. Good luck."

That evening in the mess hall I managed to be seated next to my Engineering Colonel. I approached him cautiously. He was secretly amused at my discomfort. I think it softened him regarding my problem.

"Sir, I have a problem. I have to coordinate all my activities with the other Chaplains through Chaplain Koder's office. It's almost impossible for me to work without doing so. I understand you don't wish him to get in touch with me anymore. Uh, . . . would it be all right if I contacted him?"

He smiled. "That sounds reasonable. After all, what happened this morning wasn't your fault. You were just following my orders."

"Thank you, sir." I felt I was off the hook, but realized I'd better walk carefully since there were fundamental problems to deal with. Now I clearly understood the difference between Line and Staff authority. Both Chaplain Koder and I knew he had no right to "issue orders" to me, although he was one man who enjoyed exercising his rank. He had only staff authority. He had no tolerance for anyone who did not cow-tow to him. In actuality, he had had little formal army experience. He had risen to the rank of Lt. Colonel while serving in the reserves at home. This tour was his first active-duty full-time experience.

I called his office the next morning and talked to his Assistant to coordinate my activities. No further mention was made of the incident, although the Chaplain made no attempt to initiate contact with me directly at any time in the future.

I also got the feeling that Chaplain Koder did not like Mormons although he never did actually say so. Subsequent events tended to confirm my suspicions. I think the reason he appeared so angry over the incident was because he felt it gave him a valid reason to condemn me in some official career-damaging way for not obeying his orders, and he wanted to call attention to it. He was surprised and upset when it backfired.

Word of the disagreement between the Chaplain and the Colonel spread rapidly through the Battalion, then through the whole post. The odd result was that attendance at my chapel picked up markedly the next Sunday. I guess the men were curious to see the Mormon Chaplain who had become the center of controversy between two high-ranking leaders. In any event, I had become known all over the post.

Chapter 5.

Hunter-Liggett

Besides the Engineering Battalion, I was organizationally assigned to the Medical Battalion. One of the exercises the Engineering Battalion had was war games at Hunter Liggett Military Reserve which is located near to the Hearst Castle. The men referred to Camp Cooke as (to put it politely) "the rear end of California." It is the point that sticks out along the coastline. The weather is continuously damp and muggy. One of the things that impressed me was geraniums grew everywhere. They were beautiful, but I didn't like their odor.

Compared to Hunter Liggett, Camp Cooke is paradise. At that time of year Hunter Liggett has a temperature swing of over 100 degrees between the heat of the day at 120+ degrees and the chill of the night where it goes below freezing. I've never liked camping. My Dad forced me to do it when I was a child. He thought it was a real treat. I resisted in vain. He always actively participated in Scouting. He was an Eagle Scout and many years a Scout Master. Much to his chagrin I made sure I never became even a Tender Foot.

When the Engineering Battalion completed its two-week exercise at Hunter Liggett and returned to Camp Cook, I told everyone how happy and relieved I was that it was over. The explanation given for going there was that it was the place in the United States where weather and terrain conditions most closely resembled the situation in Korea. As a result I dreaded the idea of being sent to Korea.

Right after we returned from Hunter Liggett, I was told that I would be going back there for another two weeks with the Medical Battalion. Here I was, the only person in the two battalions that got a double dose of the place. I thought it was ironic. Perhaps the Lord was trying to teach me patience and obedience. In any event, I didn't have a choice. I had to be patient and obedient, so back I went.

I made the best I could of it. It was tolerable. The guys were pleasant. The food was good. The exercises were demanding, but not too demanding. I figured I'd survive. And I did, but not in the way I anticipated.

We were playing war games. The idea was that the enemy forces (Blue Team) were to try to invade us (Red Team) and wipe us out . . . and we were to invade them and wipe them out.

I had taken my jeep and trailer. My trailer had a tarp that completely covered it. I had a mattress in the trailer. At night I would pull the tarp over me and have one of the men fasten it down at the corners. The cold weather was miserable. Every morning I would wake up and find the tarp covered with frost.

Near the end of the tour I awoke one morning and hollered for someone to come and loosen the fastening on the tarp so I could get up. A Sergeant opened it and "reported" to me. I soon learned that during the night our battalion headquarters had been successfully overrun by the Blue Team and all our officers and most of our enlisted leaders had been "killed." The enemy had not expected anyone to be sleeping in the trailer, so I was the only officer in the whole battalion that was still "alive."

The men naturally assumed I was in command. I explained to the Sergeant that "Chaplains do not have command." He countered that "you are the only officer living so you have to take command." I told him "Carry on, Sergeant, and find out how serious the damage is." He took charge and did a fine job. That was the extent of my command.

When I returned to my Engineering Battalion headquarters at Camp Cooke, the Adjutant winked at me knowingly and said, "I understand you know how to bivouac better than any of the other officers in the Medical Battalion . . . and you wound up in command. Pretty good for someone who couldn't make tenderfoot."

That night in the mess hall the officers toasted me. I hated the whole situation. I had become well known all over the post . . . again. Later whenever anyone brought the subject up, I would just say, "the good Lord was watching over me." The Division Chaplain seemed to like me better after that.

Chapter 6.

Getting Married

One of the true highlights of my tour at Camp Cooke occurred when Marguerite called and said she and her Aunt Blanche were coming to the neighboring town of Santa Maria for a week's visit. I could see her!

It was wonderful. We managed to have three or four dates during that week. We decided to get married at the earliest opportunity. It looked as if I was inevitably headed for assignment in Korea, only no one knew how soon it would happen. We figured I would not have the opportunity to get home to get married unless I could arrange for a temporary leave in order to attend General Conference in Salt Lake City the first week in October.

I applied for the leave. It was approved, so we laid our plans accordingly. I would travel home on Wednesday. We would get married on Thursday. That gave us Friday, Saturday and Sunday to attend conference, and drive back to Camp Cooke the following couple of days. There is an advantage to getting married at the time of General Conference. You never forget your wedding anniversary.

We were married for time and eternity in the Salt Lake Temple on October 2, 1952. It was a very happy occasion. Marguerite had overcome her doubts, and we were ready to start life together.

We held our reception the next day. It seemed like everyone important in our world came. All our family and loved ones, our friends, and just everybody was there to wish us well. Even a lovely lady I had met and baptized in the mission field traveled all the way from North Carolina to obtain her endowments in the temple and be present at our wedding. It was very special to me to see her there. Her name was Ava Gardner Speight. Her niece, one of Hollywood's most glamorous stars, had been named after her.

The next couple of days we attended conference in the Tabernacle, then we departed for Camp Cooke. As we drove out of Salt Lake City we enjoyed the feeling of being on our own.

When we arrived at Camp Cooke we stayed at the Guest House. This was a temporary quarters that could accommodate us for only a couple of days. Before leaving for Salt Lake City I had not been able to find more permanent accommodations.

We ate at the mess hall. That was a new experience for Marguerite. She was not accustomed to eating from tin trays served from steam tables. She was a good sport. In fact, she seemed to enjoy it. She commented about how good the food was and how much there was of it.

She spent the next day looking for a place to stay. She found a room in Lompoc. There was a lovely widow lady named Mrs. Barnes who rented us a room she had added at the back of her house. The thing I remember best about it was it had a tin roof that clanked all night when it rained. It rained often.

Lompoc is the flower seed capitol of the world. In 1952 a double-page centerpiece in Life magazine featured a field of Snapdragons over 248 acres in size that formed an American Flag. We drove to the top of a hill that overlooked the field. It was breathtaking.

I could get off post almost every night by signing out VOCO. Meanwhile the room where we were staying had no cooking privileges. Just outside the post's main gate there was a fast food stand where we liked to stop for hamburgers. It had a juke box that played current favorite records of the day. One of the songs we played most often was Jo Stafford's "You Belong To Me." The words seemed to fit our situation.

Marguerite made friends with an LDS couple that lived in Lompoc. She would spend most of the day with the wife, Florice Thomas, who had been a missionary in the same mission I had served in. Her husband was a guard in the federal Disciplinary Barracks in Lompoc.

A Ward in a nearby city was having a Halloween Dance. We decided to go. We did not know anyone in the Ward. It was a costume dance, so we tried to think of something appropriate to wear. Marguerite came up with the idea of dressing as ghosts. We could have sheets that covered us almost completely. She cut eye-holes in them and we went. Hers had big eyelashes drawn on it, so everyone could tell she was a lady ghost. I found a huge artificial cigar about 18 inches long that I pretended to smoke at the dance. Smoking is prohibited by the church. It did not go over very well with the Ward members. They were all wondering who this strange couple was. I was wearing army boots so they suspected we were from the nearby military post. We never did unmask or let anyone know who we were. I felt it was a bit naughty, but it was fun.

Not everything was fun at Camp Cooke. Every weekend many of the men would rush to Los Angeles, a distance of a couple of hundred miles. Many of them would get drunk then drive back to the post. The traffic was heavy and dangerous. Almost every weekend someone from the post would be killed in an accident. Too many times it was someone from my outfit. When that happened, as Chaplain I had the duty of notifying their families. That is one of the hardest things I ever had to do.

I recall one time in particular. We got word that one of our men had been killed. His Company Commander called me. He and the man had been friends back home in Illinois for many years. We went to the man's home together. His wife was just setting dinner on the table. She was worried because her husband was late. Their two small sons were already sitting at the table. As we approached the house we could see them through the window.

That made it especially difficult. I rang the doorbell. The wife came to the door. She took one look at me and the Captain standing together, and promptly went into hysterics. We had to calm her down and confirm her worst fears. She kept moaning "What am I going to do? What am I going to do? How can I raise the children without their father?" My heart was breaking for her.

I spent the next few days helping her get in touch with her family in Illinois and arranging for her to travel there. Unfortunately, that was only one of several such happenings.

With another family, the man was only injured. I had to tell his wife and children he was in the hospital in a nearby city. I arranged transportation to take them there. Just before we left, I was secretly told he had passed away. I didn't know whether to tell her, or to take her to the hospital. I decided to let the Doctor break the bad news to her. I remember the horrible feelings I had as I watched her suffer while we made that trip, knowing what news was waiting when we got there. In the end it was a good thing we made the trip. We were able to make the funeral arrangements and take care of many necessary details while we were in town. She took the news better than I expected. I think she had prepared herself for the worst as we were traveling. I had been able to tell her he'd been thrown completely out of the cab of the truck by the impact of the collision. A whole civilian family had been killed in the other vehicle.

I would drive into Los Angeles about one weekend every month to visit Jim Hickman. When I first reached him on the phone I had the impression that we had stopped mid-sentence fourteen years earlier, and then simply picked up our conversation where we left off. It is good to have this kind of friendship.

Returning from one of those trips late at night, I was getting drowsy. I thought of all the traffic accidents and decided I should stop driving when I was so tired. I chose a motel in one of the small towns about 100 miles from camp. In the middle of the night I dreamed I was back on a train. The bed was rocking badly. A peculiar noise brought me fully awake. The bed was still rocking. The earthquake continued a few more seconds. An electric wire outside my window flashed brightly and made a buzzing sound as it was stretched and broken in half. A similar sound was what had awakened me. This was the earthquake that centered near Tehachapi, California in 1952.

It was about two weeks after this event that I was conducting an evening Sacrament meeting for the LDS group on post. We had finished taking the Sacrament and were singing the second verse of a song when a young soldier came in the back door of the chapel and motioned for me to leave the stand, come down and talk to him. "This is most unusual" I thought as I continued leading the singing. He motioned desperately again. As we finished the verse I stopped the song and indicated for my Assistant to take charge while I went to see what was wrong.

This young soldier was not a member of the church, but he had known where to find me. His fiancé was on the phone. He asked me to talk to her.

I picked up the phone and said "Hello." She was almost incoherent. I asked her what was wrong. She cried, "They won't let me see him. They're going to send him overseas into the war. They won't let him come here to see me, and I can't get permission to come on the post to see him. I'm going to kill myself!"

I looked at him. He looked young and helpless. Despair was written all over his face. I told her she could come to the Chapel. I would arrange for her to get through the main gate, and she could see him here, now. I called the main gate and told them to let her through as she had an appointment with me.

Exactly fifteen minutes later she was in the Chapel. She had come a distance of twenty miles while she was in such a badly agitated state of mind. I got the two of them together, then I let her have the scolding of her life. The memories of the families I had had to notify of deaths due to traffic accidents were painfully fresh in my mind. She must have been traveling over 80 or 90 miles an hour on twisting canyon roads. She was not only endangering herself, but anyone else who happened to be on those roads.

"You aren't going to be any good to anyone, including him, if you're lying dead somewhere along the highway. If you're old enough and mature enough to get married, you better start acting like an adult!"

She calmed down quickly. I left the two of them to talk together while I went back to the meeting. After the meeting they thanked me for helping them to get together and work things out. I had only been married a few weeks myself, so I could empathize with how they felt.

Chapter 7.

Lompoc Disciplinary Barracks

Among my other assignments was one to go to the Lompoc Federal Disciplinary Barracks once a week and meet with the LDS men that were incarcerated there. It was a federal prison that ranked with Leavenworth, Alcatraz and other formidable places.

The first time I went, I experienced real apprehension. It is frightening to hear six steel doors, one at a time, clang shut and click behind you as you walk in. You say to yourself, "thank God they'll open when I want to leave." You have a feeling of despair and empathy for the inmates as you walk down a hallway past rows of cells. Most of them were empty because the men were out in the courtyard at the time I arrived. The steel bars looked very thick and unyielding. Everything was either cement or painted a similar dull and depressing gray.

The guard conducted me to the prison chapel. There were eight men waiting for me. I recognized them as brothers in the gospel who were in awful circumstances. My heart went out to them. I saw to it that each one had a copy of the Bible and a Book of Mormon. I went through my missionary lessons, one each week. We partook of the Sacrament. I learned the story of each one and gained an understanding of what had happened that brought him to such a place. Each time we prayed together I felt the presence of the Holy Spirit. It was a revelation to me how much our Heavenly Father loves each one of us, no matter what we've done and where we might be.

As a result of this experience I now better comprehend how much the sacrifice of our Lord meant regarding forgiveness after we have repented.

There was one young man in particular that I befriended. He was there because he had committed murder. I tried to find means to console him without condoning what he had done. He held the office of Teacher and had been inactive since he was a teenager. He began reading the Book of Mormon in earnest.

When it came time to leave the meetings, I remember my feelings as I approached each one of those six steel doors. The guard who accompanied me would signal someone I couldn't see. The door would magically open and we would walk through. It was always a relief to reach my car in the parking lot and drive away.

The few remaining weeks at Camp Cooke passed quickly. Soon I received orders to go to Fort Lewis, Washington in preparation for departing to Korea.

I'd suspected that the Division Chaplain had not liked me because I was Mormon. In the foyer of my chapel we had racks that contained literature from all the churches except the LDS church. Despite protests from my Assistant, Corporal Gary Forsey, I had refused to put our tracts out among the others for public display. I would hand them out personally when someone requested them. I made sure everyone knew I always had them readily available.

After I arrived in Fort Lewis I received a letter from Forsey. The Chaplain who replaced me at Camp Cooke was Baptist. He discovered the LDS tracts I'd left behind and put them in the racks. The following Sunday the Division Chaplain came into the chapel and saw them there. He promptly made comments about "too much denominational literature" and removed all the tracts from the chapel leaving the racks completely bare. The next day he returned and loaded the racks with literature from his own denomination exclusively. Then he issued an order that all tracts in all chapels would be handled through his office. The Baptist Chaplain was outraged.

Chapter 8.

Fort Lewis, Washington

Marguerite and I drove up the coast highway through California and Oregon toward Fort Lewis. It is beautiful country. Yosemite Park and the Redwoods are so impressive it is hard to describe their grandeur.

A couple of nights we traveled in such heavy fog that we couldn't see more than three feet in front of the car. There was little or no traffic on the two-lane road. We felt truly alone.

When we arrived at Fort Lewis I checked in at the appropriate unit. It was a temporary situation most men passed through on their way to Korea. I wasn't sure how long I would be stationed there. It turned out to be thirty three days. It rained thirty of them. Rain is an expected way of life at Fort Lewis, and this was the rainy season.

We were assigned quarters in a barracks building. We had a spacious three bedrooms with lots of wooden pillars that reached to the ceiling, minimal cooking facilities, a table and chairs, and six army cots. We pushed two of them together in one of the bedrooms. There were a couple of inches difference in their heights. The floor was wooden planks with dust-filled cracks between them. Even with the furniture we had, the place looked empty.

However, it wasn't empty long. It soon became the center where LDS servicemen gathered. There was always someone staying with us overnight or just hanging around during the days. We made many new friends and had an enjoyable time.

It was the Christmas season. We went into Tacoma and Seattle to do our Christmas shopping. I remember Seattle as a city where I couldn't get my directions straight. The blocks are in triangles or some other configuration quite different from the square patterns in Salt Lake City where I grew up. I wondered why anyone would lay out their city like that. The square pattern makes it so much easier to find your way around.

We were shopping in one big department store. We agreed to meet in half an hour at the main entrance. Without her knowing it, I secretly spied on Marguerite as she bought some presents for me. It was fun watching her. Later, after I had opened them on Christmas and expressed appropriate surprise and pleasure, she confided that she was aware I was watching her so I hadn't fooled her at all. I don't think she watched me when I bought her presents, but I guess I'll never know for sure. She always did outsmart me.

Christmas eve we had a tree. We also had an apartment full of homesick men who made the best they could of a party together.

One other valuable lesson I learned at Fort Lewis. Never underestimate the power of the enlisted men. Even though a man has a low rank as far as the army goes, he still manages to maintain his authority as an individual. I relate this story as an example of something humorous, yet it has its darker side.

There were two clerks in the Classification and Assignment office. They constantly complained to me about the Warrant Officer who headed their group. He was brusque, difficult, overbearing, and self-important. He was also overweight and out of shape. Nothing they did seemed to satisfy him. He was slack in the way he carried out his own duties, but demanding in the way they fulfilled theirs.

One day they confided to me what they'd done. They'd cut orders on him, assigning him to go to Korea. They put it in a stack of other orders he was to sign. He signed everything without reading any of it. His signature made all the orders official. Suddenly he found himself on his way overseas to the battlefront. He protested that it couldn't be correct. Nevertheless, it was official, and off he went. They told me they now had someone much more pleasant to work with.

From that moment I learned that the clerks who did the actual details like typing and filling out forms were the ones who got the job done. This proved to be very beneficial throughout my entire army career, as I shall show later. I also learned that I should read everything carefully before I signed it.

Section III.

Korea

Chapter 9.

My introduction to Korea

We drove home from Fort Lewis to Salt Lake City. After three weeks of leave, I kissed Marguerite goodbye and caught the airplane that would carry me on the first leg of my trip to Korea. The flight to Korea was long and tedious. This was before the jet age. The plane had four propellers that droned on and on and on throughout the next few days and nights.

We stopped briefly to refuel in Kiska, Alaska and Cold Bay on the Aleutian Islands. It deserved its name. The runway had a layer of ice about three inches thick. It was so slippery I had trouble standing up. One of the attendants told me that it was never clear of ice, not even during the summer. I dislike cold weather. I was glad I was not going to be stationed there.

The plane skidded during its takeoff, which was no surprise, just a little disconcerting. Soon we were safely in the air and the droning of the engines resumed. I recall looking down at the expanse of the Pacific Ocean. At night there was nothing but absolute blackness . . . blackness as far as the eye could see in any direction. I thought how awful it would be to go down into that, and have to wait for help to come from a thousand miles away.

After hours and hours of flying I saw a pinpoint of light. Then another. Then a few more. Finally there were lots of lights. They became more and more plentiful until there was a whole panorama of them. We were approaching Japan. What a welcome sight. Edison, thank you! I treasured the results of your work more at that moment that any earlier one I could remember. It was another hour or so before we landed at the big airport in Tokyo.

We got off the airplane and were quickly transferred to another one to take us to Korea. I remember looking at the other men who had left their homes and loved ones. Their faces showed their worry and resolve. None of us knew what we were getting into, who would be coming home, when, and in what condition. Everyone put on a show of good spirits, but the underlying dread was evident.

It was a relatively short flight to Korea. My first impression was, it's the only land I could smell before I could see it. It had the foul odor of an out-house. The Koreans use human excreta as fertilizer. They carry it in buckets hung on a yoke over their shoulders. These were humorlessly called "honey buckets". I thought, "What a dismal, backward place!"

I have no idea where we landed. From there I was put on a train for somewhere else. That night was one of the worst of my life. The train had been shot up. It looked like it had survived some of the fiercest fighting of the war. There were bullet holes everywhere. Most of the walls and roof structure had been blown away. There were no windows left. The cold February air blew freely through the car.

Korea is a peninsula that lies between two seas. When it's winter, it's a moist, chilling cold. It passes through you like no other cold I've experienced. I sat in the car with my hood over my cap, and my parka zipped up around my ears. I was snuggled down into the seat as far as I could get in order to avoid the chilling wind. Finally, the train began to move causing the wind to circulate and make it seem even colder.

Snow and ice covered the ground. The only things visible were the railroad tracks that ran alongside the ones we were on. "Well,

Lord, I told you I would go wherever you wanted me to go. You certainly decided to test me this time." I sat there shivering.

I heard a child's voice. I must be dreaming. There are no children on this train. I had an aisle seat, away from the window. The man next to the window nudged me and indicated I should look outside. What a shock!

There were children running beside the train in the snowstorm. They were either naked or practically so. Most of them were tiny tots not over three or four years old. The oldest appeared to be about ten. They were shouting "Hello! Choc-o-late!" "Hello." "Hello." "Choc-o-late." These seemed to be the only English words they knew.

I was distressed to see children, barefoot, running along the steel rails in the freezing cold. Snowflakes swirled around them. "Oh, God, how can this be? What am I doing here? What am I supposed to do?"

The men on the train began throwing whatever food they had to the children. Most of what they had were cans of K-rations. They threw the can openers and hoped the youngsters would know how to work them. Some of the men threw parts of their uniforms and other items of clothing. Everyone was affected by what they were seeing. It was an initiation for all of us. What a welcoming committee to our new home! Well, at least we weren't directly involved in the shooting war . . . yet.

After spending the night in that cold Hell, I arrived at the Replacement Depot in Yong-Dung-Po. After a couple of days I was informed that I had been assigned to the 84th Engineer Battalion at Moon-san-ee.

Moon-san-ee had been a city of more than 40,000 people. It was near the 38th parallel about 35 miles north of Seoul. There was absolutely nothing left except the battered rusted vault of the former bank building. There were evidences of foundations of other buildings. Nothing else. I thought, "what complete devastation."

No Korean civilians were permitted above a certain boundary mark which lay miles behind me. If any were caught in the area they were shot and then checked for identification. There was nothing in the area except open fields on which a few weeds and grass had begun to grow. If I had been a tourist casually traveling through the area and had not known better, outside of the bank vault I probably never would have suspected there had been a city there less than three years before.

Chapter 10.

The Pressures of War /
The Adjutant's Suicide

I arrived at my new Battalion. Everyone seemed pleased to see me. It was an Army unit located like an island in the center of the 101st Marine Division.

Behind us was an Artillery unit that kept firing "Long Toms" at the enemy. When those guns fired, the earth shook. You could hear the shells whistle as they passed overhead. Then you could hear the boom when the shell exploded in the distance. I was told the guns had a range of about seventeen miles. You could tell roughly how far away the shell exploded by the interval of time it took from the firing until you heard the sound of the explosion.

Once in a while you could hear a distant cannon fire, then a shell would explode behind us in the area of the Artillery unit. It took me a while to get used to shells passing overhead both ways. I prayed often that there would not be a "short round." I lived in that circumstance for about six months. During that time neither side fired on my unit.

My battalion was engaged in building the X-Ray Bridge. That was its code name during construction. Ultimately it was renamed the Libby Bridge. But I shouldn't get ahead of my story.

The Bridge was two lanes wide, made of steel reinforced concrete, about 78 feet above the surface of the river at high tide, and about a quarter of a mile long. It had seven spans that were supported by eight concrete pillars. The foundations of the middle pillars rested in the water. It turned out to be the biggest bridge ever built by an Army engineer group under combat conditions. It crosses the Imjin River. This river is unique. When the tide comes in from the sea, the river flows upstream. There is as much as a 35 foot difference in the water levels between high tide and low tide. Part of the day the water flows downstream and part of the day it flows upstream.

During the construction of the concrete bridge we had a pontoon bridge next to it that floated on the surface of the river. That was the only means for crossing until the big bridge was completed.

About once a month the enemy would lob a shell onto the riverbank near our motor pool just to let us know they had us zeroed in and could hit us anytime they wanted to. Nevertheless, they never fired on the bridge itself, nor on my unit. It seems they wanted the bridge completed as much as we did. However, we had no knowledge or assurance that they would continue withholding their fire. Nervous time.

I was green. I'd had little experience in working with so many different personalities under the kind of pressure we were experiencing. The chaplain who preceded me had been a member of my class at the Chaplain School so I knew him, but not well. His name was Boecher which was only one letter off from the spelling of my own name, Beecher.

I was assigned to the tent which comprised the Headquarters Company's officers BOQ. The battalion had only a couple of buildings. Everything else consisted of tents. The buildings were the mess hall and the Officers' Club. The latter was very small. Both buildings were of temporary construction. Because we were an Engineering Battalion, we could construct accommodations that were better than what most other kinds of units had.

I soon learned that the Chaplain was the one person most of the men felt they could rely on and share confidences with. I learned early to keep my mouth shut, listen carefully and keep confidences confidential. For example, my first day there, one of the company commanders pulled me aside and confessed he had had the Colonel in his rifle sights twice that day. The Colonel had been making "unreasonable demands on the men." When this company commander had gone to the Colonel with the message that the men were tired of working twenty-four hours a day, unhappy and almost ready to revolt, the Colonel called for a Battalion formation and berated the men badly and embarrassed this commander and several other officers in front of the men. It was fairly well known that the Colonel had piles. His most offensive comment to the commander regarding the men was "My ass bleeds for them."

That happened before I had met the Colonel. I didn't know what to expect. At mess that night he called me over to his table. He wanted to get acquainted and sort of sound me out. I got the impression that the former Chaplain had been a problem to him. He did not seem particularly pleased to see that this skinny young Chaplain was fresh out of Chaplain School and this was his first "permanent" assignment. Then again, perhaps it could be to his advantage that I was so green, so he could do whatever he felt he needed to do without my interfering.

He struck me as gruff, short spoken, but very sincere and dedicated to getting the bridge built. His attention was clearly focused on that one objective no matter what it took to get the job done. It didn't matter to him if the men liked him or not. "This is war, not a popularity contest." I found myself in agreement with him, yet there might be better ways to handle it. It was especially important to me because I was the morale officer of the unit. And morale was not good.

The Battalion consisted of six companies: Headquarters company, and A, B, C, D, and E Companies. They were scattered across a small valley within a two mile radius of each other. The

Bridge was located about a mile and a half away from the Battalion headquarters.

My "Chapel" was a tent located on one slope of the valley. It had enough folding chairs to accommodate about 100 people. There were over 900 in the Battalion.

My office was another tent on the opposite slope of the valley about a city block away from the Chapel. The furnishings in my office consisted of a couple of badly beaten up folding chairs and a desk. The desk was a wooden door resting on two wood whiskey crates. That was okay with me, I didn't spend a great deal of time there anyway. We also had a few more whiskey crates so we could offer a seat to anyone who dropped in. This led to an amusing confusion.

I don't know how the word gets around, but somehow my parents back home in Salt Lake City heard that I was drinking heavily. When I sent them photos of my office that showed it was furnished with whiskey crates, it confirmed their worst fears. Their letters of admonition were delightful. It took me a while to get them to finally understand that Boecher, not Beecher, had accumulated those crates. I merely inherited them from him.

There were several LDS men in the unit, including our Dentist, Dr. Wallace Paull. He and the doctor became good friends of mine. They stayed close together a lot of the time.

As morale officer, I got to drive to Seoul to the Special Forces Office and pick out the movies that the men watched in the Mess Hall after dinner. I also drove there about once a week on various missions.

My first week there I was called and told to report to Chaplain Drake at the 8th Army Chaplain's Office. He was the Adjutant for that office. He was a very kindly gentleman, what you would expect a minister-chaplain to be like. He always had a worried or flustered air about him. He was trying to coordinate the work of all the Chaplains in Korea. He had his hands full. We enjoyed each other's company. He wanted to know what ecclesiastical supplies I needed and so forth.

I had been with the battalion about three weeks. One evening as I returned from Seoul I was confronted by the Dentist and the Doctor. They were extremely upset. The battalion Adjutant had shot himself in the mouth. The Dentist had been the first person to reach him. "I saw the light fade from his eyes as he died. The Colonel deliberately set out to drive him to it!"

I realized this was a time to shut up and listen carefully. Chaplain Boecher had heard about it and come to the unit during the day. He'd had a very stormy session with the Colonel and left before I returned. He and the Adjutant had been best friends. The Adjutant left a wife and two small sons.

The Adjutant had always been friendly and helpful to me. I respected him. He struck me as being capable and able to cope. He did drink quite a bit, however, I hadn't expected this to happen.

I tried to learn everything I could about the situation. Later that evening I received a phone call from Chaplain Drake telling me to come to the 8th Army Chaplain's Office the next morning. When I arrived he said, "We need to know everything that's going on in your Battalion. Yesterday you told us everything was okay, now this! Sit down and write out a complete report of the incident and make clear the Colonel's role in the matter."

I told him, "I'm not ready to put anything in writing. I don't have all the facts." He told me "the former Chaplain has accused the Colonel of outright murder. The Doctor and Dentist have sent in extremely damaging reports supporting that position. We need your confirmation as present Chaplain that such is the case."

I told him "I'm not ready to make such a statement. In the first place, the Colonel treats everybody the same. I don't think he's a vindictive man who sets out to drive people to suicide. He's trying to get the job done the best way he knows how. Further, I have no way of knowing what was going on in the Adjutant's mind. Neither do the Doctor or Dentist."

Then I reminded Chaplain Drake that he couldn't give me a direct order to write any reports, so I wasn't going to write one until I was sure I had the facts straight. Even then, I would probably give him only an oral one.

I felt terrible about the Adjutant's death. I felt for his family. He was a brilliant man who'd been thrown into a war. He'd taken the brunt of the conflicts between the Colonel and the officers who served under him. In my opinion not all the pressure had been exerted on him from above. There was plenty from below as well.

When I got back to the battalion the word had already reached it that I had refused to condemn the Colonel. That was my first lesson on how fast the grapevine works in the Army.

The Doctor and Dentist came to me. "How could you stand up for him? You know how he is! What's the matter with you?" And so on. I got a lot of pressure from them and from several other officers as well. "This was our chance to get rid of him, and you blew it!"

"I did the best I could. I'm not going to say anything officially until I have all the facts. I've been around the Colonel. You've been around him. None of us are about to commit suicide. Do you honestly believe he set out to drive him to it?" They responded with a stormy "Yes" then turned their backs and left me. I sat there wondering if I'd done the right thing. Something inside me said "Yes."

It was a couple of days later. The Colonel and I had occasion to be alone. He said, "I understand you stood up for me." I replied, "I did what my conscience told me to do. I desperately want to do the right thing, and I don't believe the things that were being said about you." I was not trying to butter him up. I could have destroyed his career. There was no reason to try to butter him up and he understood it.

He said, "You majored in management in college. What am I doing wrong?" I was impressed with his directness and his honesty. He was a good man trying to do his job.

"I hope you won't be offended, but here's what I've seen. When you give an order the men seem to resent it. They resist anything you say. Meanwhile your Executive Officer is extremely popular. He goes around telling jokes and acting like a hale fellow well met. If you were to bring him aside and tell him what you want, and have him give the order, it would be accepted smoothly. I think he would enjoy the increased responsibility and authority. No disrespect, Sir, but if you keep a relatively low profile for a while I think everything can settle down without the work being disturbed." I didn't tell him the Executive Officer bad-mouthed him behind his back.

"Thank you, Chappie. I'll think about it." That was all he said. However, he did begin using the Executive Officer to deliver his orders. It was interesting to see that the Executive Officer soon quit bad-mouthing the Colonel and began to better understand the situation under which he'd been working.

Chapter 11.

"Teach Us To Read"

I worked hard at being what I thought was a proper Chaplain to the men. I went down to the bridge to watch the men working with the heavy machinery. Some of them wanted to show me how to operate it. I protested that I'd never done such a thing and it was way beyond me. They laughed and insisted I try. I got into the seat of a huge bulldozer and tried to run it for about half an hour. It went into reverse unexpectedly. It wouldn't raise the earth-moving scoop when I wanted it to. I couldn't even find the right gear. I had a terrible time. I wash-boarded a wide area so badly it took them almost an hour to repair the damage. They all laughed at my expense and loved it. Here was a college graduate who couldn't do what these school drop-outs did every day. It was a humbling experience.

That evening at Mess I was sitting at the table when the Colonel sat his tray down beside mine. "I understand you learned to operate a bulldozer today" he said with a smile. I was not happy about it. "I wouldn't call it that. It was a disaster."

"The men loved it. It was one of the best things they've enjoyed in weeks. Keep up the good work." Then he pointed out to me that most of the Chaplains who preceded me had hardly mingled with the men, but kept to themselves in their "office." I'd always felt I was expected to be with the men of the unit so I could get to know each one of them individually, by name. I'd learned a great deal about many of them, their families, their hopes for when they returned home, etc.

Later that night something unexpected happened. I was at my office when a group of about 15 men came in. "Chappie, will you teach us how to read? We never got very far in school, and we figure you can help us." It was one of the highlights of my service experience. Because I'd admitted I couldn't run heavy equipment the way they did, and they could teach me, they were willing to come to me and admit their problem and ask for my help.

"You bet I will! I'll get some beginning reading material and we can hold class at least three evenings a week. Okay?" "Okay."

Class began. As it turned out several of them were from North Carolina where I'd served my mission. We soon found out we had a lot more in common than we'd suspected. One of the fellows was from Kinston. He had a last name I recognized. I asked him if he knew Pat and Carrie. "Those are my parents!" I had visited his home. That really broke the ice with all the men.

Attendance at church picked up. Eventually we added a second tent, then a third. Finally we needed enough seating for 300 people. We didn't have that many chairs, so the guys made some benches. It was great to be able to bring the gospel message to that many homesick, overworked men.

The rainy season set in. Water collected where we had tied the sides of the tents together in such a way that the three of them became like one large room. One Sunday morning just before church I saw the roof sagging badly under the weight of the water. Jenkins, my assistant, and I tried to open it up so the water could drop through. Suddenly it did. A real deluge caught us unprepared. I had to rush back to my quarters and change into dry clothes. So did he. We got back in time to start church, but barely on schedule. The chairs and benches in that area were soaked so several of the men chose to stand in the back rather than sit on them.

The rain continued. I remember one night I was sleeping with my arm outside my sleeping bag. I touched the side of my tent. It was so wet and cold it woke me up. I lay there listening to wave after wave of the downpour. That night it rained eight inches.

The next morning I had to go to the bridge. Large sections of the road were built on graded areas that were at least six feet higher than the surrounding fields and rice paddies. Our companies had stationed men about every 40 yards along the road so you could see where to drive. The water came to above the knees of the men who were standing on the road. You could not see where it dropped off six feet into the paddies. The water level was a uniform height everywhere and the sunlight reflected off it in such a way it was like driving on a mirror.

Not long after that Jenkins had fulfilled his two-year tour in Korea and was eligible to rotate home. I had inherited him from the previous Chaplain who, I am happy to say, had made an excellent choice. Now I was able to choose a new assistant for myself. I found Doug Wixom, an LDS man from Blackfoot, Idaho. He would be able to attend all the LDS meetings in surrounding areas without being bored while waiting for me. Doug was absolutely reliable, capable and outstanding in every way.

Since Chaplains are not permitted to carry weapons, my assistant had to be someone I trusted with my life when we were traveling. Doug seemed the best choice. I asked the Colonel for him, and he was assigned to me. The Captain of his company was upset.

"Chappie, he's the best heavy equipment operator in the whole battalion. Chaplain's assistants are supposed to be misfits. How'd you happen to choose him?"

"My assistants are always the best men I can find. I have enough problems come my way without my looking for them."

"Well, okay, Chappie, but you owe me one."

Father Rice, a Catholic chaplain from the Marine Division, held Mass for my men. In return I would meet with the LDS marines. My duties with the LDS men were much simpler than his duties in holding Mass for my men.

Each LDS group was well organized. Each had its own Group Leader, two Counselors, a Secretary, etc. if there were enough men in a given area to create a formal group. My role was to coordinate with the military authorities to provide them with whatever they required to hold their meetings. The requirements were relatively simple. They consisted mainly of having bread and water for the Sacrament, which they usually obtained for themselves, hymnals, perhaps an organ, and a designated place and time, plus permission from their various units, to meet.

The Armed Forces Hymnal does not contain all the usual songs of the LDS church, although it does have several traditional ones that we use. I would make special requests to the LDS Servicemen's Committee at church headquarters for our regular LDS hymnals. Bruce McConkie was my contact.

It was my duty to oversee the groups and make sure the Group Leaders were functioning, and they were holding meetings on a regular basis. When someone rotated home, I helped select new leaders. I had thirteen groups under my supervision, or might I better say, observation.

One of the LDS Marine groups was on the other side of the river about a mile away from the bridge. Whenever I went to meet with them they were scattered into several fox holes. They would crawl carefully to gather into one large foxhole for the meeting. They told me to keep my helmet on and my head down. The enemy troops were so close that if you lighted a match a rifle bullet would zing in. There were some sincere prayers offered under these circumstances.

The craziness, or should I say quirkiness, of war became especially apparent to me at that moment. Here we were in a fox hole, afraid to light a match because it would cause a rifle bullet to be aimed our way, and we could look back at the bridge only a mile away. It was lit up with floodlights, spotlights, and flares more brightly than any carnival I had ever seen so that the men could see to work around the clock, and the enemy never fired on it.

While we were there we heard several of the Long Tom shells burst not far away behind enemy lines. Even while holding church services the war was always with us.

When Father Rice held Mass for my battalion, he brought his Marine assistant to help him conduct the meetings. He had an accompanist from our unit who played the portable organ for his services. The accompanist rotated home, just the way Jenkins had. We searched the unit. There was no replacement to be found. I asked Chaplain Rice if he had someone he could bring from the Marine Division to play for Mass. He said he was given only one assistant, and he didn't know how to play.

Finally I offered to play for him. I was playing the organ as well as preaching in the Protestant services, so why not play for Mass. "Would that be acceptable?" He looked surprised, then said it would be fine as far as he and the Catholic church were concerned.

The next Sunday morning at Mass when the Catholic men came into the tent chapel, there I was, playing the prelude and the songs for singing. Every one of them did a double take when they first saw me sitting there. The meeting went well.

That night at dinner the Colonel sat down beside me. He was Catholic. To my knowledge he had never attended church during the time I had been with the unit, so I was surprised he'd heard about it so quickly.

"I understand you played the organ for Mass today. Doesn't your church object? A Protestant chaplain playing for a Catholic Mass?"

I explained to him, with several other officers eavesdropping, that technically my church is not a Protestant church. We never protested or broke away from anybody. It was started when the Lord gave fresh revelations to a young modern-day prophet."

Besides I remembered a quote from George Albert Smith when he visited my mission field in a conference in Colfax, North Carolina. He said, "If you can make a man a better Catholic, do it. He will be a better man. If you can make a man a better Baptist, do it. He will be a better man. If you can make him a better member of any church, do it. He will be a better man. When he is ready for the fullness of the gospel, he will come to us."

I had no doubt that my church authorities would approve of my playing the organ for Mass. After all, they did not object to my holding Protestant services, and I'm not a Protestant any more than I'm a Catholic.

It impressed me how much better I was accepted by the Catholic men in the battalion after that. They all spoke to me when we passed each other. They even started coming to me more freely with their personal problems. It seems that if Chaplain Rice accepted and worked with me, they felt at liberty to do so as well.

Chapter 12.

Chaplain Bagley

There were nine other LDS Chaplains in Korea at the same time I was there. One of them, Chaplain Bagley, was assigned to the 2nd Engineering Battalion that was the sister battalion to mine. These two battalions made up the entire 2nd Engineering Group. He was stationed in Yong-Dong-Po which was nearer to Seoul than Moon-san-ee, where I was. I kept in close touch with him. He was from Salt Lake City. He had studied to be a Dentist before he joined the army. About once a week I would go to see him or he would come to see me.

During my Protestant sermons I was careful to use only the Bible in presenting my subject matter. The LDS Church has additional scriptures in the form of the Book of Mormon, Doctrine and Covenants, and the Pearl of Great Price. These books shed a great deal more light on gospel subjects. However, as long as I am speaking to people who have not accepted them as scripture I feel it is only being fair to them to use the scriptures they have accepted, namely the Bible. Besides, all of the LDS doctrines can be proved from the Bible.

One Sunday I spoke about Pre-mortal Existence. To my knowledge it is not taught as a doctrine in any of the Protestant churches. It is something that most of the men had never heard about in a formal service, although almost everyone accepts as fact that we all came to earth from our Father in Heaven. I was merely trying to confirm that fact.

I told them that according to Job, God the Father had called all of His spirit children together for a great Council in Heaven. He told us about His plan for our eternal progression wherein we would have the opportunity to grow and become more like Him. His plan called for the creation of the earth, and for His children to go to the earth and receive mortal bodies and be tested. Based upon our growth and obedience we would receive the opportunity to return and live with Him eternally in various kingdoms. The Apostle Paul referred to these kingdoms as degrees of glory. He described them in his epistle to the Corinthians as Celestial (which he compared to the glory of the sun), Terrestrial (which he compared to the glory of the moon, and a third degree which he compared to the stars (as one star differeth from another in glory, so also is the kingdom of God.) Our individual rewards are based on how each one of us fulfills the requirements of His plan voluntarily according to our increased knowledge and obedience.

Jehovah, His first born spirit son, stepped forward and volunteered to execute the plan. He stipulated "the glory be thine, Father."

A second spirit son, identified in Isaiah's writings as "Lucifer, the son for the morning," also stepped forward and volunteered to execute the plan. But he stipulated that "not one spirit will be lost. They will all obey thy will exactly because they will not be given free agency to make their own choices. And, for all this I shall have the glory."

The Father said, "I will send the first."

There was war in heaven, as described by John in Revelations. Lucifer rebelled and a third of the host of Heaven followed after him.

Jehovah began the work of creation. Lucifer and the spirits who followed him were cast out of heaven to the earth. They became known as evil spirits in the scripture because they were not willing to comply with the Father's chosen plan. They had given up their opportunity to receive physical bodies and to continue their growth.

Later, when it was Jehovah's turn to live His life as a mortal known as Jesus Christ, some of the evil spirits begged Him to allow them to possess physical bodies, any physical bodies, even the bodies of swine, they were so desperate.

This explains why John wrote in his gospel that Christ created everything. It also explains why most of us say babies "came from heaven", and Grandpa "returned to God" when he died.

Although many churches do not accept the doctrine of the pre-mortal existence, it is plainly discussed in the scriptures. Whether they accept this doctrine or not, most churches speak of "returning" to God. I've always wondered, if the churches don't accept Pre-mortal existence, how do they explain that someone can "return" to God, to a place where he has never been before?

I've learned also that most people believe this doctrine regardless whether their church teaches it or not.

Chaplain Bagley happened to come to my unit for a visit later that afternoon. One of my Protestant men quietly pulled him aside and asked him about it. "Was there such a thing as Pre-mortal Existence?" Chaplain Bagley assured him there was. "Does your church believe in it?" "Yes, we do." Without asking to which church Chaplain Bagley belonged, the man felt reassured that I had given Protestant doctrine in my service that morning. After all, it was all stated in the Bible.

One of the more pleasant things that developed was our choir. About 25 men came one or two nights a week to rehearse the music we wanted to use in the next Sunday's meeting. A real bonding developed among us. Having this participation greatly added to the spirituality of the meetings. Several of the officers began attending church regularly.

One weekday afternoon Chaplain Bagley came to visit. We were in my office. He had the habit of sitting low in a chair, literally on the back of his neck with his legs crossed so that one ankle rested on the other knee.

Suddenly the earth shook with a terrific BOOM! Instantly he was standing a good eight feet across the room from his chair. "What was that?! What was that?!"

I told him to relax. "That was just the Artillery unit behind us firing their Long Toms at the enemy. We call it 'outgoing mail.' It goes on all the time, around the clock."

He paused. "Is there ever any . . .'incoming mail'?"

"Of course" I answered, "all the time. Only they never fire at us, just at the units behind us. They want the bridge completed as much as we do."

"How can you be sure of that?"

"Well, to be honest, we can't be sure of it. However, that's the way it's been ever since I got here."

"Goodbye, Beecher. I'm going back to Yong-Dong-Po. It's been nice seeing you. I wish you good luck. I hope it holds out." With that he was gone. I felt abandoned because he cut his visit so short.

Every night a small rickety North Korean observation plane flew over our position. We called him "Bedcheck Charlie." You could almost set your watch by him. I often wondered why no one bothered to shoot him down. Everybody knew where he would be and at what time. Anyway he passed over us that night at his usual 7:00 o'clock time.

A very short while later we heard a terrific explosion and the sky lighted up in the distance behind our lines.

The next morning we learned that a major ammunition dump, located next to Chaplain Bagley's unit in Yong-Dong-Po, had been blown up. I drove down to see him. He looked frazzled and haggard. "Didn't you get any sleep last night?" "Are you kidding? How can anyone sleep with an ammunition dump blowing up next door? It kept going on all night as the explosion of one thing triggered the next. The worst was when it first started. I thought the world was coming to an end."

"You should have stayed up there with me, where it's peaceful." His reply was a look that said it all.

It was about three weeks after that that Chaplain Bagley came to see me again. It was a beautiful spring day. We decided to take a drive around the area. My assistant had something else to do so I drove my new jeep. It seems that I had already had two jeeps destroyed in accidents, but that's another story.

We traveled around the countryside and enjoyed seeing the open fields. It was the first time we had actually seen anything green. Most of the foliage had either been destroyed in the battles that happened before I arrived in Korea, or the civilian survivors had burned everything that was left in an effort to keep warm during the winter. This trip was a real treat.

We had gone about twenty miles when we came to a Guard standing near the entrance to a side road that led to one of the Marine units. We pulled up and asked directions about how to get back to my unit.

The young guard had a peculiar look on his face as he approached us. "You're both chaplains?."

"That's right."

"Do you carry any weapons?"

"No. Why?"

"And you just came down that road?"

"Yes."

"How far down that road have you been?"

"About twenty miles."

"Did you see anything . . . unusual?"

"No. Why do you ask?"

"You've been behind enemy lines the whole time. I'm the point man."

Bagley and I quickly got directions on how to get back to my unit on safe roads, and headed there immediately.

I'll never know how the word got back to them that fast, but that evening at Mess several of the officers teased me about our sight-seeing tour. "Boy, it's a good thing you're a Chaplain and the Lord looks after you." I could only agree with them.

The Executive Officer said, "From now on, whenever you go anywhere, you are to have your armed Assistant with you."

All I could say was "Yes, Sir. You're absolutely right."

That was the last time I drove my own jeep.

I was very humble in my prayers that night. It seems the Lord had indeed been watching over us.

That was not the end of it. Both of us were called in by Military Intelligence to give a full report of everything we had seen. Actually there wasn't anything to report except a clear road, newly sprouting green grass on the fields, and a beautiful afternoon. The Intelligence officers seemed delighted that the absence of the enemy from certain areas was confirmed by first hand observation, although it was evident that they considered what we had done was both risky and stupid. We were in no position to argue.

I was also called into the 8th Army Chaplain's Office and given a stern lecture by Chaplain Drake about not placing myself in dangerous circumstances. I presume Chaplain Bagley got the same treatment although we never discussed the matter.

It was an odd feeling, but because of this adventure some of the men in my battalion, particularly some of the ones in our choir, began to treat me almost as if I were a good luck charm. In confidence I had told one of them about the blessing I had received when I was set apart as a chaplain. Evidently he had spread the word to some of the others. Several of them commented privately to me that they wished they could have someone with the authority of an Apostle of the Lord to have given them a similar blessing.

There was another time my Assistant and I got lost while driving around. We were reasonably certain we were not in enemy territory, however there's no denying it, we were lost. As we drove along we saw in the distance an extremely tall guard wearing a turban. Obviously he was from India. There were units from all nations around us. As we pulled up to the guard to ask directions I whispered to Wixom, "I hope he speaks English."

The guard had overheard me. In a broad Oxford accent that made my English sound illiterate he said, "Of course I speak English, Sir." Compared to this seven and a half foot tall man, I felt even smaller than usual. He very courteously answered all our questions and we went safely on our way.

Chapter 13.

Chaplain Hammond

Chaplain Hammond, an old college buddy of mine, was newly commissioned as a Chaplain and assigned to a unit relatively close to mine. His very first day he came over to see me. I was delighted to see him and learn the latest news from home. We spent a pleasant afternoon together. When it came time for the evening meal I invited him to stay. We decided he should send his Assistant home to his own battalion and we would drive him back later.

We enjoyed the meal. After the mess hall was closed, it was converted into a "theater" and movies were shown. My Assistant usually ran the projector. I had an appointment for counseling with several of the men, so I suggested to Chaplain Hammond that he watch the movie for an hour or so, I would meet him at the movie and then we would drive him to his unit. He agreed.

I finished my appointments and headed for the Mess Hall. The movie was just ending. I asked Wixom where Chaplain Hammond was. "He left here about 45 minutes ago. I thought he was going to the chapel to see you."

"No. He didn't come there." We spent the next hour and a half searching for him. We looked in the chapel, back to the mess hall, over to my BOQ, to the Officers' Club, back to the chapel. All over the compound. We finally had everyone in the Battalion alerted and looking for him. He could not be found anywhere. It was now well after midnight.

I spent a sleepless night worrying about him. The first thing the next morning Wixom and I drove over to his unit to see if he had returned. There he was, safe and sound, and unconcerned about my concern for him.

"Where did you go?"

"I decided it was a beautiful moonlight night, and since my unit was only a couple of miles away, I decided to walk home."

"Why didn't you tell anybody you were leaving? We had the whole place looking for you until after midnight."

"Wixom was busy with the movie, and you were at the chapel. It didn't occur to me."

"Great! Did you happen to take any short cuts through the fields, or did you stick to the main road?"

"I stuck to the road. Why?"

"You saw all those little red triangles hanging on the barbed wire fences that surround the fields?"

"Yes."

"Do you know what they mean?"

"No."

"They mean the field is mined with napalm. You'd have been burned to a crisp in only a couple of steps!"

"Really . . . ?"

"Really! Now, what was the password last night?"

"Password?"

"Did you happen to see any guards or guard gates along your way?"

"No." I didn't see anybody until I got back to my unit. Besides, if I had I would've explained to them that I'm Chaplain Hammond."

"Oh, sure. You're going to walk up to a Korean guard who doesn't speak English, whose been taught to shoot anyone who doesn't say the right password phonetically, and explain that you're

Chaplain Hammond. According to orders he'd shoot you dead, then they'd check to find out what you were doing there."

"He'd do that?"

"Of course. Those are his orders. Do you know where the enemy units are? They're pretty close by in case you happened to take a wrong turn."

"You know I'm new."

"Did you check your weapon before you left unattended?"

"You know we don't carry weapons. Do you carry one?"

"No. I don't. But I keep my Assistant close by me, and he has one. I understand that Chaplains are the favorite targets of the enemy. They especially like to capture them."

"You mean I have to learn a different password every night, and stick to the main roads?"

"I suggest you stay tight inside your own unit until you learn the routine around here. I was scared to death for you last night. It seems that the good Lord watches over us, no matter how stupid the things we do are."

I didn't tell him about what Bagley and I had done, but somehow he got the idea that I had learned from personal experience how serious the danger he had faced had been.

I did tell him about the experience one of the other LDS chaplains had had. It was reported to me that within the first couple of days after Chaplain Ben Mortensen, who had been in my class at the Chaplain School, arrived in Korea, his unit had been under concentrated attack. Eighty-five percent of his men were either killed or wounded. Chaplain Mortensen was in the middle of a major firefight. He took his consecrated oil and administered to the men lying on the battlefield, regardless of their religious affiliation or extent of their injuries. Who could take time to check dog tags to see if a dying or injured man was Catholic, Protestant or Jewish while bullets were whizzing past his head?

This was an example of truly exercising your Priesthood. He was heroic. I prayed I would never be in a situation like that. Thank God I never was, although I was sometimes in something relatively close . . .

Chapter 14.

Dr. Piccione / M.A.S.H.

Our original Doctor rotated home. His replacement was a cool character who'd formerly served in the Emergency Room at Chicago General Hospital. I admired his ability to keep calm in stressing situations. Never once did I ever hear him raise his voice.

About once a week some unit nearby would be attacked by the enemy and suffer extensive casualties. Among them was a Turkish unit, about a mile away. They were powerful men and fierce fighters. I was told that once one of them had drawn his formidable looking knife from its scabbard he could not replace it until it had drawn blood. If not someone else's blood, then he would use his own.

On more than one occasion Doctor Piccione would awaken me in the middle of the night and say "Chappie, we are needed." I would get up immediately and accompany him to the nearest first aid station.

These were makeshift arrangements where wounded men would be brought for first aid, or should I say "initial treatment" to save their lives before moving them to better facilities. Sometimes these were M.A.S.H. hospitals, sometimes they were more rudimentary. It depended where we were taken to deal with the emergency. Usually helicopters or trucks were used to transport the injured men. After initial review they would probably be sent to a Hospital Ship that lay off the coast a couple of miles under the protection of the U.S. Navy.

My usual role was to try to comfort each young victim while the Doctor cleaned and bound his wounds. I would mop their brows and try to keep their minds off their injuries, if they were conscious. I recall one young black marine who had an ugly rifle bullet beneath the skin of his wrist. You could clearly see it. The bone had been shattered.

Another young red-headed marine had an ugly open hole in his abdomen where a rifle bullet had entered. We had to put a bandage across it and tie it there to stop the bleeding.

One night the Turkish unit next to my own unit was hit. None of them spoke English, so my role in comforting them consisted of helping to wash and bandage their wounds.

The situation in the MASH Hospital is not like most people suppose. The men have been blown up in explosions or shot and lying in mud so their wounds are dirty and infected. The mud is not ordinary mud. It is mud from the Korean rice fields that have been fertilized using human excreta. The smell of the burned flesh, the blood, the infection, the stinking mud, the crying of the wounded, the confusion as new wounded men are brought in, and as the bandaged and dead ones are sent out to the waiting trucks or helicopters, make it as close to Hell on earth as anything I can imagine. As a result, I've never watched the hit television series called "M.A.S.H." Somehow it didn't seem to me to be a logical premise for a comedy. I also got the impression that its set was a more permanently located site with more equipment and materials than the first aid type stations I helped in.

Every time such an attack took place, I thanked my Father in Heaven that it had not been my unit. I realized it easily could have been. The units that were hit regularly were on the right, left, and behind my unit.

In the middle of all this, the Colonel and the new Doctor didn't get along with each other. The Doctor indicated many of our men were showing the strain of working too hard, too long hours, too many shifts, etc. He began giving the men a medical reprieve for a day, or half a day, when he felt they needed it.

Soon there were lines in front of his tent-office in the mornings. I talked to him about it and warned him that the Colonel and some of the company commanders were beginning to resent his giving so many permits, and asked him if he was sure they were absolutely necessary in every case. "It's slowing down the work on the bridge." Despite the bad feeling between the Colonel and the Doctor, I never heard either of them say anything out loud about each other.

One night the telephone in our BOQ rang. The Doctor answered it as usual. When the phone rang between the hours of 1:00 a.m. and 4:30 a.m., we assumed it was for the Doctor. He listened. Hung up. Then called our Dispensary. I heard him very, very quietly and deliberately say "Go take our little ambulance, pick up our little patient, and bring him home to our little dispensary. Do you understand that?" I could feel the anger seething under the quiet, slow phrasing he was using.

The situation was this. One of our men had become ill that day. The Doctor had examined him and determined there was not anything seriously wrong. However, he'd warned the man he would probably have a relapse before he started feeling better. While the Doctor and I were away at the MASH hospital that evening, the relapse occurred. One of the Medics under the Doctor's immediate command became worried. Instead of notifying us and keeping the man in our Dispensary until we returned, he took him to a nearby Marine unit's dispensary. When we got back early that morning the Doctor received the phone call from the Marine Dispensary. That was when he called our Dispensary and told his man to go pick up the patient. When the Medic got to the Marine unit's dispensary, the patient had already been sent out to a Hospital Ship off shore.

The next morning the Colonel called the Doctor in and made it clear he was "unhappy the Doctor had not given adequate treatment to our man." He explained that if the Doctor would "tone it down and become less generous in dishing out permits to miss work each day, I might be willing to overlook it and not write an official reprimand since this is your first offense."

The Doctor was furious. He responded by saying, "if you're trying to compare the judgment and competence of a Medic against my years of training and experience at Chicago General, go ahead. Write your report. You'll find I'm right and you'll have embarrassed yourself!"

The Colonel became angry and began shouting. The Doctor kept his voice very quiet. In the end the Colonel did not write the reprimand, and he was glad he didn't. After the man had been forwarded from the Marine unit dispensary to the medical ship, they'd given him many tests. Their team of doctors determined that what was wrong with him was exactly what our Doctor had diagnosed in the first place, and the treatment he'd recommended was 100% correct. The Colonel learned the next day that the Doctor had already notified the 8th Army Medical Headquarters that the Colonel had been interfering with his work. After that the Colonel did not try to play one-ups-man-ship with the Doctor anymore.

The next morning before our Dispensary opened, there was a line of about 100 men waiting at the door. I went in to see the Doctor and asked, "Is this what you wanted?" He responded "I know the Colonel's not going to give me any more static. Don't worry, Chappie, I'm not out to sabotage the bridge. If a man doesn't have a legitimate complaint, I'm not going to give him a pass. I value my medical reputation more than that."

I want to make one additional comment concerning the Doctor. He was of Italian descent. He was the first person I ever saw who made Pizza . . . and they were delicious.

Chapter 15.

Marine M.P.s

My battalion of Army Engineers was like a small island completely surrounded by the 101st Marine Division.

One day Wixom came to me with a complaint from most of the men who drove vehicles for our Battalion. The Marine Division MPs had been issuing an extraordinary number of traffic tickets to them for speeding, or whatever other violations they could dream up. It was a convenient way for them to achieve their quota of traffic tickets without damaging the careers of fellow Marines. Meanwhile it was causing havoc with our men. Our drivers were getting Article 15s, losing their stripes, being reduced in rank, having fines levied almost daily, and some had even been court marshaled. Several had been given stockade time for multiple offenses.

I told him there wasn't much that I could do about it, but "I'll talk to the company commanders to see if they can think of any ways to remedy the situation."

I met with the Adjutant and the Executive Officer. Their reaction was "If tickets are issued, that's the end of it. The Companies will have to handle it."

It was a week later that this happened. Through no fault of my own, previously a couple of Jeeps that had been issued to me were totaled. Therefore, when I got this new Jeep, the Colonel warned me "If it happens again, you're going to be walking the rest of the war." I knew it was an empty threat because in addition to going to the Marine Division and other units to hold religious services, I had to go to Seoul every week to report to the 8th Army Chaplain's Office, and also pick up the movies for the Battalion.

At least I hoped it was an empty threat.

He had a governor placed on the new Jeep so that it could not travel faster than 25 miles an hour. The Colonel had personally ordered the Motor Pool officer "Keep that governor right where it is. I don't want the Chaplain getting into any more accidents."

Wixom and I were driving into Seoul. It was raining softly. We were both wearing helmets and panchos and had no insignia showing. We'd gone about half way when a Marine Jeep zoomed past us. It splattered mud all over us. Since we were dressed for the rain, it didn't matter, but it was irritating. We got the impression the driver had done it on purpose.

About ten miles down the road we came to the Checkpoint. To our surprise the Marine guard signaled us to pull over and stop instead of waving us through like he usually did.

There was a Marine Warrant Officer who informed us we had been "clocked at 65 miles per hour." He proceeded to hand Wixom a traffic ticket for speeding that had already been prepared before we arrived. All he had to do was fill in the name.

I protested "There must be some mistake. There was a Marine Jeep that went past us at high speed, but it's impossible for us to travel at that speed."

He became hostile. "You better mind your own business and keep your *** **** mouth shut or I'll give you a ticket too." I told him, "This is my business. This is my driver. We weren't speeding."

At that he became profane and abusive. It quickly escalated into an argument during which he swore at me with the foulest language a Marine could muster. We almost got into a fist fight. I took off my pancho and helmet and was ready to go at it, although I weighed 128 pounds and he weighed about 260.

When I took off my pancho he paused, looked at me again and said in amazement, "You're an officer!" I was thoroughly upset. "What's that got to do with it?"

"Sir, I'm sorry I spoke to you the way I did."

"That has nothing to do with it. You have no right to speak to anyone the way you did. I'm going to file charges against you for disrespect, and anything else I can think of that applies in this situation."

He looked again. "You're a Chaplain!"

"That's right. And I don't lie. I told you we weren't traveling any 65 miles an hour in the 30 mile zone, and we weren't."

"I'm sorry, sir, your driver is getting this ticket anyway."

"Good. Give it to me. Your people have been giving my people tickets illegally and unfairly for weeks now, and I'm going to see what I can do about it." I snatched the ticket from him and we drove to the Marine Division headquarters. Secretly I was happy we didn't get into a fist fight. He would have pulverized me. Besides the difference in our size and condition, Marines are trained for hand-to-hand combat, and chaplains are not. Wixom was standing by with a look of complete dismay on his face.

I looked for Chaplain Rice to get his help in the matter. He was away. So we went to the Division Chaplain's office. He and I had worked together on a couple of previous occasions. I told him about the ticket situation and the Warrant Officer's swearing and abusive attitude. I also pointed out how my men had reported being subjected to the same kind of treatment, minus the apology when he discovered I was an officer.

Next, I stopped at the Marine Division Provost Marshall's office. I had met him earlier through Chaplain Rice. He was most cordial and pleasant. I told him about the problem we were having with our men receiving unfair tickets from his MPs. "I'm sorry, Chaplain, if that's happening I'll look into it, but in the meantime this ticket stands. The people in your judiciary will have to handle it."

I told him about the Warrant Officer's swearing at me, and said I wanted to file official charges against him. He gave me some forms. I filled them out.

When we were in Seoul we picked up the movies. Then we stopped at the 8th Army Chaplain's office and told Chaplain Drake I wanted to fill out forms and take whatever legal action was necessary to make the complaint stick against the Marine MPs who were giving out tickets unfairly and illegally to my men. I also wanted to file an official complaint against the Warrant Officer for his swearing. "Maybe the men will begin thinking twice before they engage in all this foul language if an example is made and they realize it's illegal to use it."

Chaplain Drake readily agreed with me. "I shall bring it to the attention of the 8th Army Chaplain himself. He'll bring it to General Westmoreland's attention. Meanwhile, you should drop by the 8th Army Provost Marshall's office and let them know about it." So I did.

Again, news travels fast on the Army grapevine. When I got back to my unit that evening, barely in time for dinner in the mess hall, the Executive Officer walked up to me with a half smile and said, "I understand you had a little trouble with the Marine MPs this morning, Chappie."

"I sure did." About that time the Colonel sat down by us. "You know I've been telling you those MPs have been unfairly giving tickets to our drivers, and you've been taking away their stripes and giving them Article 15s as a result. Well, now I can give you proof." With that I took Wixom's ticket out of my pocket. "See, right here in black and white it accuses us of doing 65 miles an hour in the 30 mile zone."

"So . . . ?"

"So, Colonel, you remember you had a governor put on my Jeep so it couldn't go over 25 miles an hour. That governor has never been touched or tampered with. Come on out and drive it yourself. It can't go over 25. It's mechanically impossible. Now we have the proof of what they've been up to. A lot of our men have been punished unfairly."

The Executive Officer said, "Well, if they issue tickets, there isn't much we can do about it except follow through and let each company judicial officer try each case on its own merits."

"They haven't been trying cases. They've been handing out blanket punishments. You should look into it and rescind all those bad Article 15s and restore their stripes. Are you going to continue letting those MPs do their damage?"

The Colonel was rather enjoying watching his Chaplain and his Executive Officer working on opposite sides of the issue. Finally he spoke up.

"What do you suggest we do about it, Chappie?"

"I've done about everything I can think of today. I filed official complaints with the Marine Division Chaplain's office, the Marine Division Provost Marshall, the 8th Army Chaplain's Office and the 8th Army Provost Marshall's office. And if that doesn't get results, I intend to write to my Congressman and the Associated Press."

The Colonel looked uncomfortable. "My, you have been busy." He gave the Executive Officer a knowing glance. He had a surprised look on his face as well.

"I've got the proof. Go drive it yourself. Now are you going to quit giving people Article 15s on the basis of the MPs words alone. A man is innocent until proven guilty. I spent a couple of years in law school and that's a well established principle. I haven't heard of a single instance where a Marine MP has been hauled in here to testify in regard to any of these tickets."

"Now, now, Chappie. Let's not make a federal case out of it."

"I'm mad enough to. You should have heard the way that Warrant Officer swore at me! On second thought, maybe you shouldn't. I've filed official charges against him too."

The rest of the dinner was eaten in relative silence . . . just some usual small talk.

The next morning Wixom was late coming to the office. He started the conversation with an explanation. "We had our usual daily formation with all the drivers who got tickets yesterday."

"What happened?"

"The Top Kick lined us up, called us to attention, and said, 'All right now, be good boys. Dismissed.'"

"That was it?"

"That was it. No Article 15s, no fines, no nothing. The guys crowded around me afterward and said, It's a good thing you had that governor on your jeep. Now somebody believes us.'"

Evidently what I had done got someone's attention in high places. The number of tickets given our drivers dropped so dramatically that the men were joking about it. One of the drivers confided in me that he had tried speeding and the Marine MPs had just turned their backs and ignored him. I told him "That isn't what I wanted. I was trying to make it fair, not get our people the opportunity to break the law." He laughed, and said one of the Marine MPs who was a personal friend of his from back home told him his Marine Sergeant instructed their men "Be careful before you give any tickets to the 84th Engineers. It might be their Chaplain in disguise."

I never did learn what the outcome was regarding the charges I filed against the Warrant Officer for swearing. I presume nothing happened.

It seems like whatever you try to do, it backfires. I felt like the Doctor did when he had the long line of "sick" men wishing to have the day off. Now I had drivers who felt they could get away with breaking the traffic laws. I also thought to myself, "isn't it too bad people will put more trust in the 'evidence' of a little mechanical contraption under the hood of my jeep than they will in what their drivers or even their Chaplain says."

Chapter 16.

Movies: Marilyn Monroe or Mickey Mouse?

The next thing that came up was Wixom and the men in the Choir complained that a few of the men who watched movies in the Mess Hall after dinner were making obscene comments during the shows. They expressed it in these terms, "They're turning the air blue. You can't believe how bad it is."

I felt like a fool trying to nursemaid a bunch of rough and ready army engineers. Nevertheless I decided to see what I could do about it.

Ordinarily Wixom ran the projector for the movies. We had a couple of other men who were trained to take over when Wixom and I were away from the camp. That wasn't often, but it did occur from time to time. There was a huge black Mess Sergeant who took special care to keep something prepared for us so we could expect to have a warm meal waiting when we returned. He regularly attended church and basically was one of my good friends in the battalion. He stood more than 6'7" tall and weighed well over 300 pounds. I might add, there wasn't much of it that was fat. If I were ever in a fight, he was one man I would want on my side.

On the evening in question, I entered after the picture had started and listened to see how bad the situation was. It was bad. I took over the projectionists' job. I sat by the projector and wondered what I should do. After a brief silent prayer for guidance, I decided to shut it off.

Everyone sat in silence for a few minutes, then a voice said "Turn that *** **** projector on!" I answered "I will when you clean up your language." There was a long uncomfortable pause. Then several voices said, "On with the ******* movie!" "Not until you're ready."

Several people began to get angry. Things escalated. The whole thing came to a climax when the big Mess Sergeant came and stood over me and demanded, "Just who do you think you are?" I responded, "Turn on the light and see."

He pulled the light chain. The light went on. He had the biggest fist I have ever seen poised in the air just above my head. I thought to myself, I'm going to have black eyes for a week. The Sergeant took one look and literally wilted. "Oh . . . good evening, Chaplain." He said it so obsequiously that it was funny. Everybody broke out laughing and the tension was off. He continued meekly, "How long have you been here?"

"Long enough! I come in here often to share the movies with you. I've had a lot of complaints about the comments some of you are making, and I agree. They're uncalled for. As you know, I'm the one who goes to Seoul and brings back the movies. I can choose Marilyn Monroe or Mickey Mouse. Which one would you rather watch for the rest of the war? I don't think Mickey would generate any obscene comments. Would you like me to remedy the situation that way?"

An unknown voice said "You'd be surprised at the comments you'd get if you try that, Sir." Everybody broke out laughing again. I was happy the tension was off. Humor is a wonderful cure for tension. The men worked hard. The shells continued to whistle over our heads. The units all around us continued to be attacked. We were never sure when our turn would come. We needed all the relief from tension we could find.

"Okay, you guys. I won't try that. But keep it down, will you please?" I turned the projector back on, sat a few minutes, then left quietly.

Later that evening the Executive Officer and I were sitting in the Officers' Club. "I understand you gave the men a lesson in politeness this evening." The officers were always needling me. I guess it had something to do with the fact that I was so tall, so skinny and so young. They seemed to be amused as they watched to see what awkward situation I would get into next. However, they all seemed to like me because I was trying hard to do the best job I could.

"I've been getting complaints from men who don't enjoy hearing obscene remarks during the movies. It was getting bad."

"I heard the Mess Sergeant almost knocked your block off."

I responded, "You never saw such a big fist in all your life."

The other officers who were sitting nearby started laughing. One of them said "I'd give $10 just to have seen the look on his face when he saw it was you." I had to agree with him. "From my standpoint, it was worth it."

After that a lot of the men teased the Sergeant about (almost) clobbering the Chaplain, but he remained one of my good friends anyway.

One afternoon when we were alone in the Mess Hall he said, "I'm sure glad I turned on that light and looked before I hit you. I'd have been in the stockade for the rest of my career." I told him, "Sarge, you're not half as glad as I am." Even he had to laugh about it.

A couple of weeks later I was talking to Wixom. We'd brought back "Niagara" starring Marilyn Monroe. He told me the following happened. One of the men made a very obscene remark during the movie. Everyone shushed him immediately. "Be quiet. The chaplain might be here!" Wixom said, "You've got everybody royally spooked. That Mickey Mouse comment really worked. They think you meant it."

"That's not what I want. I hate having that kind of reputation." Then I thought to myself, "that is funny . . . being able to threaten a tough fighting bunch of Army Engineers . . . with Mickey Mouse."

Chapter 17.

Korean Civilians

In addition to the problems our drivers were experiencing with the Marine M.P.s, there were some that arose in connection with the civilian population. No civilians were permitted in our general area. But, whenever we drove to Seoul or other locations south of the zone, the roads passed through their villages.

The Korean people had no respect for the kinetic force of a moving vehicle. They ignored them, or were completely unaware that they existed.

I recall sitting beside the driver of a 2 ½ ton truck while it followed an old Papa-son for almost five minutes as he leisurely strolled down the middle of the roadway. The driver had the air-horn blasting at ear-shattering volume. The old man didn't notice. Finally the driver inched forward very carefully and barely touched him with the front bumper. He turned, saw the truck and in shocked panic began screaming. He came completely unglued. Magically 40 or 50 people appeared around the old man from the surrounding houses. There was a lot of arm waving and excited hollering in Korean. It took almost ten minutes to calm everybody down so we could continue our journey.

I said to the driver, "Do you suppose he was deaf?"

"Naw. They've even walked straight into the front of my truck when they were facing it and never seemed to notice 'til they touched it. I had my lights on and the air horn blowing, and it still didn't phase them."

I don't understand that mentality. It seemed like the sense of touch was their only means of communication. Sight, smell, and sound didn't work. Most of our men called the Korean nationals "Gooks".

My initial impression was one of bewilderment. How could anyone not notice a huge truck with its air horn blasting? For several months my contact with the Korean people was limited to seeing them as we drove by. Frequently I would see three men working one shovel. One had hold of the handle. He would push the blade into the ground with his foot. Then he and two others, who were holding onto two ropes that were tied low on the handle, would pull the shovel up with its load of dirt. I can't dream up a more inefficient way of working.

On the other hand, the officers in my unit had Korean houseboys who made up their beds, washed their clothes, shined their boots, and kept things neat and tidy in general. Two such boys worked for the officers in my tent. Their names were "Buckshot" and "Charlie".

Of the two, I felt Charlie showed more initiative. In fact, I thought Buckshot was a little on the lazy side. Usually he had to be told specifically what to do. Charlie took care of things before you realized you needed them to be done.

Buckshot worked for the Dentist and two other officers, while Charlie worked for the other three of us. Charlie was supporting his family who had been left destitute because of the war. I never knew where they were living. It was in one of the villages at least a hundred miles to the south. Buckshot was an orphan.

The dentist, Dr Paull was from Salt Lake City. He took a liking to Buckshot and told him that after he rotated home he would adopt him and bring him to the United States. Dr. Paull already had three sons. The younger ones were about the same age as Buckshot.

Dr. Paull finished his stint in the service and rotated home a couple of months later. True to his word he sent for Buckshot. He asked me to coordinate all the paperwork and arrangements on the Asian side of the ocean while he worked from the American side. Things did not progress easily. First we learned that Buckshot was not completely the orphan we had understood him to be. His mother had been killed in the war, but his father was still alive. It took over a month to locate him because his village had been demolished and no one knew where he was or how to proceed in searching for him. Buckshot knew where his Great Aunt lived in another village. She helped guide us to his father. He gave his consent for the adoption.

Then the job of obtaining assistance from the State Department fell on me. To get their permission for Buckshot to go to the United States was one of the most difficult, frustrating, and distasteful tasks I have ever tried to perform. Dealing with these self-proclaimed "Gods" from the United States State Department is absolutely impossible. The book, "The Ugly American" doesn't nearly state it strongly enough. It deals with average tourist types. The State Department people have polished arrogance and contempt to an art that exceeds the power of words to convey. Until you have attempted to deal with them you cannot imagine the disdain and contempt they hold for the rest of us mere mortals. I can't recall being more antagonized or repulsed by any other group of human beings. I felt remorse that they represented our country. In my opinion they were doing so much harm in their public relations with other countries that they appeared to be deliberately trying to offset all the good and sacrifices our military men were making. If I ever have a chance to vote on the matter I would abolish the State Department as quickly as possible.

Dr. Paull finally got his Senator from Washington D.C. to intercede. Even that carried very little weight with them, although they did take sufficient notice to acknowledge "a U.S. Senator had expressed an interest in the case." I don't know how he finally managed it, but he did. Dr. Paull got the necessary clearances and Buckshot left for the United States.

To complete the story of Buckshot, here's what happened. He graduated from high school in Salt Lake City with high honors. He received offers of scholarships from several major universities, including Harvard. He chose to graduate from the University of Utah. He went on to complete his masters and doctors degrees. He taught many years at the University of Hawaii.

This gives a better impression regarding the capability of Korean people when, individually, they are given a chance in life. I've often wondered what Charlie would have been able to accomplish if he had been given a similar opportunity.

Chapter 18.

Jeeps!

During my 14 months in Korea I had five jeeps assigned to me. They kept getting wrecked. Oddly enough, only one wreck occurred when I was present. Nevertheless, I got a reputation for having bad luck. This reputation was due partly to the Colonel's sense of humor.

One day he called for a "safety meeting" with all the officers of the battalion headquarters and the six companies. He had carefully prepared visual aids for his presentation. One chart showed the accident rates for each of the following categories: Headquarters Company, Company A, Company B, Company C, Company D, Company E and the Chaplain. I was a category all by myself. It was embarrassing. To make matters worse, I'd had more accidents than two of the companies, and they each had many vehicles.

He also enjoyed using a picture of my poor smashed-up jeep, with HQ-9 plainly showing on the bumper, on his safety campaign poster.

My last two jeep accidents occurred this way. Wixom was in my third jeep on his way to Seoul. I was not with him. He was about half way across a narrow one-lane bridge when a huge Korean Army truck drove onto it from the other end. Wixom honked the horn, flashed the headlights, and backed up until he was completely off the bridge. The truck showed no sign of slowing down or acknowledging he was there. It finally bore down on him, crashed into the jeep and forced him off an eight foot embankment. He managed to jump out just as the jeep started rolling over sideways down the hill.

The accident with my fourth jeep was also caused by a Korean Army truck. This was the one when I was present.

We were in a convoy. The highway became a long one-lane bridge over a rice paddy area. One of the vehicles in the front of the convoy broke down, so the whole convoy stopped. There was a huge "six-by" truck immediately in front of my jeep. We couldn't see past it. When it stopped we stopped.

After a few minutes we became aware of a sound rapidly coming up behind us. Wixom and I both baled out of the jeep just before a huge 2½ ton Korean Army truck smashed into the back of it and accordian-ized it into the truck in front.

I looked at the offending truck. There were about 50 civilians dressed in their usual white attire standing in the bed. They melted into the surrounding houses. I was furious. I went around to the cab of the truck.

"Couldn't you see us? We've been sitting here for almost ten minutes!"

The driver shrugged his shoulders, opened his hands, palms up, in a helpless gesture and said, "Lieutenant? Sorry. Brakes havva no."

We hitched a ride back to our unit with one of the trucks in the convoy. The Motor Pool Officer sent a vehicle to tow what was left of our poor little jeep back home. That night at the mess hall everybody, I mean absolutely everybody, knew I'd had another jeep wrecked. The Colonel called me over and said, "Chappie, if this keeps up we'll run out of vehicles. Maybe we should keep you on foot for the rest of the war."

At least I can say that nobody was ever hurt in any of the accidents.

The reputation didn't stop there. Another LDS Chaplain named Money was assigned to a nearby unit. About a week after my accident he was having dinner in his unit's mess hall. He was seated next to his commanding officer who was seated next to the wall. His driver had parked his jeep on the hillside above the mess hall. It was parked on gravel. After several minutes the jeep began sliding sideways down the hill. It hit a bump and started rolling over. It came rolling down the hill and crashed into the mess hall wall next to where the Colonel was sitting. Fortunately no one was hurt, but the meal was definitely interrupted. Between Money and myself, we established a reputation for "those Mormon chaplains."

Chapter 19.

Flying With Lt. Deardon

There was an LDS pilot named Deardon stationed with an aircraft unit not far from my own who offered to "take me up in his helicopter sometime." I had never flown in one, and I was curious.

One day he asked if I could meet him at the heliport at his unit. I asked my commanding officer's permission. He said he had no objections, so I went.

We were flying quite a ways behind the battle lines. I looked down and saw a Korean woman hanging her laundry on the clothesline behind her home. She lived in a small village. You would never know there was a war with intense fighting going on just a couple of miles away.

Unknown to me, Deardon was a tease. "What do you suppose happens if the motor quits?"

"I have no idea. I hope it doesn't drop like a rock."

"Let's find out." With that he turned off the engine.

It's amazing what can flash through your mind in just a second's time. When I was about five years old I had witnessed an autogyro accident at the Alameda, California airport. The Autogyro was the predecessor to the helicopter. My parents had left me in the car while they stood at the fence about twenty feet away to watch it take off. It had a huge four-prop propeller above it like the one on a helicopter. Other than that it looked like a small airplane with the usual front propeller, wings and tail. It did not have the stabilizing propeller in the tail like a helicopter has.

I watched as the big blades started to turn. Slowly it rose straight up in the air. It began to pull forward until it came to a position over the parking lot. Gradually its body began to rotate in the direction opposite to that in which the big top blades were turning. It turned slowly at first, then faster and faster. Suddenly it dropped onto the parked cars only five cars away from the one I was sitting in. A grandmother and child about my age were killed as the car's roof caved in on them. The pilot climbed out of the wreckage and walked away uninjured.

That crash flashed through my mind when Deardon shut off the engine. I gripped the sides of the cockpit and braced myself for the inevitable impact. "Why was he such a fool? Wouldn't he know better than risking destroying his craft just to scare me? Surely with all his experience in flying . . . " A glimmer of hope.

I opened my eyes. The blades above and behind had enough momentum that they continued to spin even though the engine was turned off. We were gently floating down toward the ground. He was laughing at my distress. After we'd lost most of our altitude he turned the engine on and flew us safely back to his unit.

When we were on the ground he asked if I'd enjoyed the ride. I told him I had. "It was more exciting than a carnival ride."

He said, "Would you like to go up with me sometime in my observation plane? That's what I fly most of the time."

I told him I would, "but no funny stuff!"

"Okay. No funny stuff."

About a month later he called. I went to his unit. The plane was a small single engine one. It had two seats. The pilot sat in the front one. The passenger sat directly behind. There was a set of controls in the passenger seat as well, so the plane could be flown from either position. There were no canopies over the seats. You were strapped in with a simple canvas seat belt.

I took my camera along because I figured this would be an opportunity to get some unusual pictures of the Korean countryside. Perhaps I could even talk him into flying over the bridge my battalion was constructing.

Off we flew. We circled around. He talked to me on the headset. "Over there are the marines. On this side is the enemy. I usually try to get where I can see their positions, yet stay far enough away that their fire can't reach me. I've had a few close calls. Once I get them located, I call directions to our artillery. That's why I'm known as a 'spotter.' We're over enemy territory right now."

I talked him into flying back over friendly territory, and in particular above the bridge so I could take some photographs of it from the air.

In a little while he began to execute a few swerves and dives. My stomach was affected accordingly. Each time he went over the top and began a dive, the weightlessness would cause my camera to float up in front of my face. I had it attached to a strap around my neck. I hoped it wouldn't fly off and get lost because I was afraid to let go of the sides of the cockpit with my hands long enough to grab it.

Finally he stalled the plane and threw it into a tailspin. We were circling with tremendous momentum and hurtling toward the ground. I was nauseated. The camera was whipping up in front of me then banging into my chest with each rotation.

He took out the control bar (joy stick) and handed it back to me. "Here. This broke off. You'll have to insert it by your feet and fly the plane from there."

I grabbed the stick. I half expected to be catapulted from the plane as I let go of the sides. I looked down at my feet. There were foot pedals, but I couldn't see any place to attach the control stick. I remember shoving the stick forward to him and saying "You take this and get us out of this spin or I'll hit you on the head with it."

He was laughing as he took the stick, reinserted it, pulled the plane out of the tailspin and flew us back to his base. My stomach was so upset I could hardly climb out of the plane, but I wasn't going to admit it to him.

Once we were on the ground I said, "I thought you promised no funny stuff."

"Did you think it was funny."

"No!"

"Well, what's you problem?" I couldn't think of an answer to that one.

Finally he said, "I'm sorry, Chappie. I just couldn't resist it."

"What would have happened if I hadn't handed you back that stick?"

"I could have pulled us out of it by using the foot pedals. Do you really think I expected you to fly the plane?"

"No. I didn't think so. But then I'm never sure what to expect from you."

He invited me to dinner. I accepted. My stomach was still up there swirling around in that airplane. I forced myself to eat. I wasn't going to let him know how badly I was shaken by the motion sickness. It was a source of great personal satisfaction to me when he couldn't eat. Although he was a seasoned pilot, he also had been affected by the aerodynamic antics he had pulled. That was the last time he offered me the opportunity to fly with him.

Chapter 20.

The Libby Bridge

As the bridge neared completion, we had our first accident. A boat filled with Korean workers was tied to the bridge by a long rope. Somehow it had capsized and the workers were thrown into the current. One worker's foot had become tangled in the rope. As he tried to free himself he was struggling to keep his head above the water. One of our soldiers who was standing on the shore jumped into the water to help him.

The problem was, the soldier got so excited that he jumped in wearing full gear, backpack, rifle, boots, everything. He sank like a stone. All the Korean workers managed to save themselves. The soldier drowned.

Right at that time the tide came in and the river began flowing upstream. We couldn't find his body. It took six days of searching before we found him about 150 yards downstream. I had to write the letter to his family and explain how he had died a hero. He really did die a hero. But if he had used sense and removed all the weight before he jumped in, he would have been a living hero.

There is more to this story than you could imagine. Although the Private was of no relation to the Colonel, he had exactly the same first and last name as the Colonel, Russell O'Grady.

We finished the Bridge. Everyone was proud of it. The 25th Infantry Division was situated across the river. The bridge was the only link that division had with the rest of our forces behind the river. In other words, it was their life line in case of a major enemy offensive. We figured 25,000 men's lives depended on it. It was a wonder the enemy had permitted us to complete it without incident. We'd suspected they wanted it as badly as we did. If they were to launch an offensive, it would be their best means to cross the river. The only flaw in their thinking was, we had two of the spans of the bridge carefully booby trapped so that we could blow them out at any time. You'd think they'd have thought of that.

I was surprised when the Army decided to hold a big ceremony to dedicate the bridge. I didn't realize they dedicated facilities. It was nice for the Battalion to receive that kind of recognition.

Before the ceremony there was a lot of discussion as to what the name of the bridge might ultimately be. It had been called the X-Ray Bridge during construction. There was the strong possibility it might be named for the only person who had given his life during its construction, i.e. the soldier who had drowned. Many of the people in the Battalion objected to this idea. They said, if it bore that name, everyone would assume it was named for the Colonel, not the Private. In my humble opinion, the Colonel had ram-rodded it through almost single-handedly. It would not have been such a bad idea, except he really was not popular.

In the end it was called the Libby Bridge after a Sergeant Libby who was killed earlier in the war at a distant location. He had nothing to do with the bridge or even that zone of the war. It was a nice tribute to a hero although there was nothing to tie him personally to the bridge.

The day for the dedication ceremony came. One after another, dignitaries arrived by helicopter. I was impressed how many there were. When we were ready to begin the actual ceremony with speeches and all, I counted 48 stars on the bridge. That means General Westmoreland wore 4 stars, General Clark had 3, Admiral so-and-so had 3, and so forth. I thought to myself, "if the enemy were to lob a shell onto this bridge now, they would wipe out almost the complete Far East command. I sure hope they don't know about this, and try it."

At the conclusion of the speeches I was called upon to give the dedicatory prayer. It was a humbling and grand moment. I was pleased the Army, Navy and Marines recognized the need for prayer. Too bad our schools at home can't enjoy the same privilege.

Chapter 21.

Peace Treaty, Peace Pagoda, and a Lady Disc Jockey

About three weeks later, in late July the cease-fire treaty was signed. The war ended. The booming of the Long Toms stopped. The bridge was finished. Things quieted down.

It wasn't long before new orders came. My Battalion was to move close to the 38th parallel and construct the Prisoner Exchange Compounds and whatever other facilities were needed at the Peace Pagoda in Pan Moon Jom.

We moved across the bridge into the Demilitarized Zone, farther north than any other American or allied unit, right next to the North Korean Army. Now, no one in our unit was permitted to carry a weapon.

We had a water point up the road. It was agreed that if the North Koreans decided to violate the cease fire and commence an attack, our water point would call on the phone and alert us as to what was happening. Such notice would provide the main body of the Battalion an estimated thirty seconds head start on the invading army. All day and night everyone was nervous about whether the enemy would continue to honor the cease-fire agreement or not.

The Exchange Compounds were rapidly laid out as simple compacted floors with tents over them. Then cots and other furnishings arrived. Soon truckloads of captured enemy soldiers began to fill them.

My impression, as I saw the trucks passing by, was that the enemies looked well fed and cared for. They were singing and shouting insults. They were tearing off the uniforms and other clothing that had been provided for them. The roadside was strewn with torn clothing and cut up new shoes and boots. I wondered how they could be so happy to be returning to such an oppressive communist regime. Hadn't they learned anything about freedom?

On the other hand, when our own soldiers were returned, they looked frail and abused. Many of them required medical attention. It was obvious they had not been treated nearly as well as our North Korean prisoners had.

I never had the opportunity to talk personally to any of our returning prisoners. I did see them being unloaded from trucks then escorted to waiting trucks or helicopters. They did not spend much time in the Exchange Compounds.

It was wonderful to have the war end. At last, no more phone calls for the Doctor in the middle of the night. The work schedule of the men became light. There was time for most of them to sit around, think, and get homesick. You feel different when there is a war on and a bridge to be built. Now the war is over and the bridge completed, what is the reason for you to hang around Korea? Why not go home?

Meanwhile our Colonel rotated Stateside and we had a new Commanding Officer arrive. He was a pleasant gentleman from the South, and a Baptist. His name was Colonel Akins. He even showed up to my Sunday services several times.

In the midst of all the homesickness there was a radio station in Seoul that played American music. The guys listened to it faithfully. I recall that Earl Bostic records were particularly popular. Patti Page had a couple of songs the men liked, namely, "How much Is That Doggie In The Window?" and the one that hit the homesickness target more directly, "I Went To Your Wedding." Joni James was another singer whose songs were among the most requested. Also Doris Day.

We all began thinking of home and how we could accumulate the necessary number of points to qualify to rotate back to the States. The point system was such that if you were closer to the battlefront, and especially within the firing area, you received more points each month than you would if you were at a safer distance back behind the lines. Now with the ceasefire, it looked like we might possibly earn fewer points each month and wind up staying in Korea longer than ever. It was a mixed blessing.

As our thoughts turned homeward, there was a particular young lady disc jockey named Wendy who played the "Mail From Home" show on the radio station in Seoul. She had an unusually sultry voice and an upbeat, pleasant personality. She would present positive messages about home, and encourage the men to keep their spirits up during these times of separation.

I did a little checking and learned she had attended the Brigham Young University. I called her at the station and asked if she would be willing to come up to my Battalion and speak to the men in person.

As Chaplain, I was regularly giving Character Guidance lectures. Although we were relatively isolated from the civilian population, we had had an upsurge in venereal disease among our drivers. Our Doctor made several caustic remarks to me regarding the need to do something about it.

I asked her to talk to the men about home, girlfriends, wives, keeping themselves morally clean and worthy to return home to their loved ones. She agreed to come and speak.

Talk about the royal treatment! When she arrived, she was the first American girl most of the men had seen in over a year. She was attractive, and she had that killer Southern lilt to her voice. On a minor scale she caused as big a sensation in my Battalion as the one Marilyn Monroe had caused a few months earlier when she visited the Marine Division. Marilyn had almost caused a riot among 30,000 marines.

Everyone in my Battalion attended my Character Guidance lecture that day. Even the Colonel and all of the officers. After the lecture the Colonel invited her to dinner at the officers' mess.

That evening, when Wixom and I drove her back to Seoul we had a chance to talk. She expressed surprise that her radio show meant so much to the men, and that she held such celebrity status. I told her she was doing a superb job of helping the men keep their standards high and remain loyal to their beliefs while they were away from home. I asked about her Southern accent. It was genuine. She was a convert to the Church who came from South Carolina to the B.Y.U. to earn her degree in journalism and broadcasting. She was doing a wonderful job of it, and possibly making history in the process.

After that she often mentioned the 84th Engineers and gave special greetings on the air to individual men who wrote to her. It was probably the best Character Guidance lecture I ever gave. Even the Doctor said he could see the results of its positive influence.

Chapter 22.

R & R in Japan

After several months each person was permitted to have a period of R & R (rest and recuperation). My turn finally came around. R&R usually meant you could go to Japan. And that's exactly what it meant in my case.

It was October. The weather in Japan was lovely. I really didn't know what to do with myself for my week in Japan, but I wasn't going to waste a precious moment of it. I wanted to see all the sights, and I did manage to see many of the famous ones.

My general impression of Japan in October 1953 was it was a nation experiencing a clash between two cultures. The classic Far Eastern, Oriental culture, and the modern Western culture. People were dressed according to one or the other. Either the classic silk kimono with big bows and a wig or western style dress which usually meant denim levis. The age of the wearer seemed to play a large part in the choice of clothing. The old form of Japanese dress predominated with people over forty. The younger people preferred the casual western style.

The land is a beautiful one. It had been less than a decade since World War II. I visited Hiroshima. The city had recovered from the effects of the atomic bomb except for certain areas which had been preserved to show how bad the devastation had been.

I went to Komakura to see the famous wooden Buddha there. It was carved and inlaid with jewels. It was the epitome of Oriental art. I personally enjoy the beauty of Oriental things. As a child it was a special treat to visit Chinatown in San Francisco. I guess the impression stuck with me.

One of the most exciting sites I visited was the Diabutsi Buddha. It's made of metal. Originally it had been inside a temple. I was told that sometime in the 1200s a tidal wave had carried the building away, but the Buddha was heavy enough that it stayed in place. The building was never rebuilt, so it has remained outdoors ever since. This Buddha is about as famous a symbol in representing Japan as the Statue of Liberty has become as a symbol for the United States. It is huge. On the Buddha's left side at ground level there is a small door. I couldn't resist looking into it. The Buddha is hollow, just like the Statue of Liberty is. Inside the door there is a staircase. I went inside and climbed the stairs. They led up to a small balcony which stretches across the Buddha's shoulders. When you stand on it you are looking toward his face. On his chin there is an altar with a book resting on it. I tried to find out what the book was, but nobody around me spoke English. It was rather fun to see the looks on the faces of everyone as I emerged from the Buddha's side wearing my uniform with the Christian Chaplain's cross on my collar.

Everywhere there were tourists with cameras. I was no exception. I was trying to capture everything on film so I could remember it and relive it later.

Mount Fuji has to be the most perfectly formed natural cone of its size in the world. In the distance it appears purple with a frosting of white toward the top. It is so artistically perfect that it doesn't look real.

I stayed at one of the beautiful hotels in downtown Tokyo. I caught the bus to the LDS Mission Home and met several friends, both old and new. When I entered the Home I had to remove my boots. That is a quaint, yet practical Japanese custom that I found both pleasant (because I like to go around without shoes for comfort sake) and practical (because it prevents bringing dirt into the house). It was also a bother because it isn't easy to put boots on and off every time you leave or enter the house.

The Mission President, President Mauss, who had served for several years was just being released and returning to the United States. The new Mission President, President Robertson, was being installed the week I visited there. It was a good time to be there. They held wonderful meetings that I attended. It also permitted me to become acquainted with the new President in preparation for coordinating a possible visit by him to Korea. More about that later.

Before I got to Japan I'd made up my mind I wanted to buy some carved ivory art objects and pearls. Much of my time was spent looking for the right things. I went to Mikimoto's, as all tourists do, and bought a strand of pearls for my wife and another one for my mother.

A couple of days later I bought each of them a Happy Coat, and a set of two pigeon blood cloisonne vases.

Everyone said I should see the sights in Yokohama, so I went there on the train. Those trains traveled fast in those days. I can't imagine what it must be like today. It was even faster than the subway in New York.

In Yokohama I found a little shop on a side street that had some wonderfully carved ivory figures of Hotei. The shop owner himself had carved them. I bought one. When I returned to Tokyo the hotel gift shop had several copies of the exact same image for sale. Theirs were slightly smaller and the ivory appeared grainier or of inferior quality to mine. The cost was approximately four times greater than what I paid, so I felt good about my purchase.

There were a couple of LDS men on R&R who agreed with me. They asked to buy mine since their time was up the next day and they were returning to Korea. I said I'd try to get them one, but I wasn't going to part with mine.

I spent another day returning to the shop in Yokohama to get their figurines. The shop owner was sold out. He explained that it took him two weeks to carve one. He would be happy to make a couple for me if I would return in a month. Naturally that was impossible since I had only two more precious days in Japan myself, so my friends had to do without. They were not happy about it when I saw them later in Korea, but they understood and appreciated that I had made the effort.

One funny thing happened when I was in Tokyo. I was walking through the lobby of my hotel when I saw an old friend from my Ward back home. I went up to say hello. He ignored me. I spoke to him directly and he signaled for me to move to a nearby alcove, so I did. He came over and said, "Earl, I'm here with the CIA. Don't blow my cover." At that time I had never heard of the CIA, and the expression about being "under cover" wasn't as well understood as it is now. I asked him what he meant. He said, "I'm on a secret assignment. No one must know who I am." So I said "Okay" and that was the end of it. I later thought it was rather amusing for someone who looked very American and stood 6'4" to be pretending he was something other than what he was . . . in Japan.

My last day there I found a carved ivory chess set in the gift shop of the hotel where I was staying. I had my heart set on getting one. I wanted a medieval pattern with armored knights, and so forth. The one I saw was very Japanese, not medieval. It depicted the Emperor and Empress, 4th century Japanese warlords on horseback were the Knights, pagodas were the Rooks, and each pair of the pawns represented a different vocation. By that I mean there were twin pawns, one dark and one light. The vocations represented were a fisherman, farmer, lumberjack, merchant, school teacher, town crier, hunter, and musician. The bishops were of particular interest. The light ones represented Shinto priests. The dark ones were Buddhist monks. It was the prettiest set I had ever seen.

Because of my previous experience in comparing prices in that gift shop with those in small shops located in areas less traveled by tourists, I knew this would be no bargain. Nonetheless, I had to have it.

In Japan if you paid the first amount the merchant asked, he would laugh at you after you left. One of the Lieutenants from my unit clearly demonstrated this to me. Our R&R time overlapped. We happened to run into each other so we went shopping together. He was of Philippino ancestry and he spoke Japanese fluently. We went to the Ginza shopping district together. He wanted to buy a camera. He bargained in English. The merchant was laughing at his awkward efforts to negotiate. While speaking to an associate in the next booth the merchant revealed his cost and what markup was his absolute minimum. The Lieutenant managed to bargain him down to the lowest possible price. The merchant acted almost distressed that the Lieutenant had become such an effective bargainer. As we were walking away the Lieutenant wished him a good day in fluent Japanese. It was fun to see the shocked expression on the merchant's face.

You were expected to bargain and bargain and bargain to make your purchase. I don't like that custom because I'm not good at it. Somehow I did manage to buy the chess set. It took the last dollar I had. It was my last night in Japan so it was okay. I was now broke and ready to return to my unit in Korea.

When I caught the military plane back to Korea, I had a surprise. The seat next to mine was empty. Soon the Division Chaplain from the 44th Division at Camp Cooke entered and sat down beside me. He treated me like a long lost brother. He was on his way to Korea for the first time. He was very apprehensive about going into war. I spent most of the trip reassuring him that it wasn't as bad as he imagined. I pointed out that with his high rank he probably would be assigned to the 8th Army Chaplain's Office or some other headquarters located securely back away from the front lines. Besides, the cease fire was in effect, insecure as it may be. I resisted the temptation to tell him stories about my MASH hospital experiences although secretly I would have enjoyed scaring him a little.

Chapter 23.

A Visit By President Robertson

It was November. The weather was beginning to get a real nip to it. The prisoner exchanges were relatively completed. The future offered nothing exciting except for a possible visit by President Robertson of the Japanese Mission. My religious services were going fairly well. I missed having my tent chapel.

Since the Battalion had moved we did not have the same kind of facilities we had at the old location because this was assumed to be only a temporary location. All religious services were held outside.

One of the thoughts that came to me during the height of the fighting was this: the Latter-day Saint church is very practical. It is designed in such a way that it can function under any circumstances. Every worthy man holds the priesthood. If battle conditions prevent gathering together into congregations for worship services, and in particular celebrating the sacrament, each man can prepare and administer it for himself. Other denominations require that the Chaplain or Minister must be present to prepare it. The members can not administer it for themselves. They must rely on the Chaplain.

I heard a story that Chaplain Parsons, who had been at the Chaplain School in New York with me, was conducting a small service when the enemy fired a shell close to where the members of the group were gathered. Everyone dived into the nearest ditch or foxhole. Needless to say, it disrupted the meeting. If such conditions had continued over an extended period of time, it would make it almost impossible for formal worship to be organized in groups. In contrast, the L.D.S. priesthood holders are independent and capable of holding their meetings when only two or three of them are together.

I went to Seoul and talked to Chaplain Drake about the possibility of having President Robertson of the Japanese Mission come to Korea. "Could the 8th Army Chaplain's Office help us prepare for his lodgings, food, transportation, while he is here?"

"I'm sorry, Chaplain Beecher, but we are not equipped to assist in any way. Unless he has V.I.P status, there's nothing we can do. Can you imagine what a mess it could become if every religious leader in the world decided to visit the men from his church and have us cover the expenses? We'd be overrun with requests. You'll have to take care of everything yourselves if he decides to come. And besides, I doubt if he can get permission."

Well, that was that. I talked to Bagley and some of the other LDS Chaplains. We tried to figure out what we could do to help get permission, and what we could do to obtain proper accommodations if he came.

I met with Colonel Slover of the KCAC (Korean Civil Assistance Command). He said there was a Guest House that President Robertson could stay in for a couple of days. "If he needs more he can bunk in with me at my BOQ. We'll take care of him somehow. However, if he wants to tour the country, we will probably have to find him civilian accommodations. That can present some problems as Army food is the only thing available that complies with suitable health standards. We'll just have to cross that bridge when we get to it. The first thing is to arrange to get him here . . . if we can."

I thought of what a wonderful missionary opportunity it would be to have President Robertson tour the country, hold conferences with the men, and possibly even speak on the radio. A few weeks passed and nothing happened. I assumed that the whole idea had fallen through.

One day I dropped my glasses and they broke. I had to wait about three weeks for the replacements. It was miserable to see the world out of focus. It was especially so when I needed to read and study to prepare my sermons.

One afternoon I received a call from Chaplain Madsen, the highest ranking LDS Chaplain in Korea at the time. "Beecher, President Robertson is arriving at the Seoul Airport this afternoon. I'm tied up. Can you meet him?"

I rearranged some commitments and managed to get to the airport just as the plane was landing. Wixom and I watched carefully as the passengers came down the ramp. There were no civilians. No President Robertson.

Wixom asked, "What do you suppose happened to him? Could he have missed the plane?"

"I don't know. It's a special army plane, not a commercial airliner. He should have been on it. Let's go inside the terminal and check to see if there's a message or anything." We went inside.

As I was walking slowly and squinting at each new arrival who was seated in the waiting room, I heard a familiar voice say, "What's the matter, Beecher? Break your glasses?"

"President! There you are. I sure did. What are you doing in an army uniform? I expected you to be in civilian clothes." He was wearing an Olive Green uniform . . . with a bright red tie.

"They said I had to wear these, so I did. The tie was my own idea."

"It's sure not regulation. I guess it's all right. It's one way people may guess you're not in the army."

We picked up his suitcase and went outside to our waiting jeep. I explained, "We've made arrangements for you to stay with Colonel Slover. Then we'll get in touch with Chaplain Madsen and all the other Chaplains and finish arranging a tour for you."

"That'll be great."

We took him to Colonel Slover's office, said "Goodbye" and returned to our unit. We arrived just before the dinner hour. The phone rang. It was Chaplain Drake from the 8th Army Chaplain's Office. He was in a panic. "Chaplain Beecher, I talked to Chaplain Madsen. He said you were the only one who knew President Robertson on sight, so you were supposed to meet him at the airport. Did you?"

"Well, not exactly."

"Not exactly!" He sounded like he was having a heart attack. "Not exactly? You didn't miss him, did you? Don't you understand? He arrived here with the V.I.P status of a four-star general! When you asked me about it earlier I had no idea he was such an important person!"

I reassured him. "It's okay. I didn't see him at first. I broke my glasses. Actually he found me."

"You did meet him?"

"Yes. We did."

"Is he there with you? What kind of arrangements have you made for him? He's supposed to be staying in the V.I.P Mansion. We have a limo here exclusively assigned for his use as long as he wants it."

"I took him over to have dinner with Colonel Slover at KCAC." Then I gave Colonel Slover's number to Chaplain Drake so they could coordinate all the proper arrangements.

The rest of the week was spent traveling to LDS conferences all over the South Korean peninsula with President Robertson. It seems that when a four-star general requests that a few Chaplains be excused from their regular duties for a week, their assigned units are more than happy to comply.

On his second night in Korea we explained to President that the phone system was so good between Korea and Japan that he could easily call the Mission Home in Tokyo and tell his wife how well the tour was going. He called. One of the comments he made struck all of us as funny. He said, "Honey, they made me a Brigadier." After he finished his call we explained that a Brigadier General had only one star. He had been given the status of four stars which put him equivalent to General Westmoreland himself.

His comment was simply, "No wonder they didn't give me any arguments when I asked for you guys to accompany me on this tour." The tour covered most of the South Korean peninsula.

It was a grand experience to be with the brethren and meet all the LDS servicemen in Korea. We held meetings for almost a week. At the largest one the attendance was 246 men. The testimonies were filled with stories of how the Lord had blessed and protected each of us, and how grateful we were to Him for it. Non-member friends came to the meetings and felt the Spirit. There were several baptisms that resulted, including two fine brothers from my own unit. Their names are Keith Alberts and Fred Gaunt.

President Robertson told of the exciting progress the Church was making in Japan and he promised it would not be long before there would be a temple in Tokyo.

Chapter 24.

Pusan / Orphans

In November a fire broke out in downtown Pusan. My Battalion was ordered to go there and construct emergency shelters for the people who were left homeless. There were over 50,000 of them in an area that covered about six city blocks. Many of them had been living in cardboard boxes. Now they had nothing.

We moved in and began bulldozing the remains of the destroyed buildings. There was an old manufacturing plant of some kind that presented a special problem. It had a couple of very tall smokestacks that had to be toppled over without hitting anyone or anything to cause new damage. It took our capable engineers a couple of days to figure that one out. But soon they had the area completely cleared.

The Red Cross and KCAC were working effectively to provide the civilian population with food and other essentials of life. We quickly began putting up tents. Each one would accommodate about forty people. It took a lot of tents. We installed shower tents and cooking tents and everything else that was needed for temporary living facilities.

My Battalion was located on top of a hill a couple of miles away from the burned area. There was a street that led from the MSR

(Main Supply Route) up to our area. For the first time since I had arrived in Korea my unit was housed in wooden buildings, not tents. We were in three large buildings that resembled barracks. There were the enlisted men's barracks, the administration or office building combined with the officers' quarters, and the mess hall. The whole area was fenced off from the street below. There was a small Guard Shack by the gate.

At one end of the Administration building there was a room large enough to serve as a chapel. It looked like it had been a classroom. There were seats, or rather benches, a counter that looked like a science laboratory counter of some kind, and a wall behind it that had previously supported a blackboard which was now gone.

Pusan had never been overrun during the actual shooting of the war, yet it looked even worse than Seoul in many ways. There were literally a couple of million refugees in the city. We were told there were over one hundred thousand lepers, and nobody knew how many other people who were affected by tuberculosis and other exotic oriental diseases that we westerners had never heard of.

Shops lined both sides of the road that led from the MSR up the hill to our Battalion compound. There were open air stalls with dried squid hanging on their wooden frameworks. The foul smell of Kimshi dominated the air.

The people were struggling to survive by any means available to them. I hated seeing how some of our men took advantage of their desperate situation. Prostitution was everywhere. Venereal disease was rampant. I felt a sense of real frustration as my jeep would drive up that road and I would see men from my unit disappearing into the buildings so as not to be seen by me.

In my Character Guidance lectures the Doctor and I both warned the men not to participate in activities that exposed them to venereal disease, tuberculosis, leprosy and other exotic oriental diseases that might not show up for as much as ten years after they got home, in exchange for a few moments of questionable pleasure now.

When you were around civilians you had to be wary for reasons other than health ones. The children had been trained to cut your pockets with razors and grab your wallet. The black market flourished. There were thousands of civilian automobiles in Pusan. Every one of them had jeep wheels. There was no legal way they could have acquired those wheels. I don't recall seeing any service stations to sell gas, but the cars seemed to have an abundant supply. There was extensive discussion regarding equipment that disappeared from our motor pool and the difficulty we were experiencing in getting newly ordered supplies. Yet at the same time, with a couple of days notice the black market could provide you with items as large as a multi-story crane or an Army Tank . . . and the paint would still be wet.

One day I received a phone call from Colonel Slover. He was now in Pusan to coordinate the efforts of KCAC in helping the victims of the fire, and the refugees in the city in general. He wanted to introduce me to Dr. Chou. Dr. Chou was an outstanding educator who was listed on the faculty of three or four of the major Korean universities. He was also the Director of a chain of orphanages in Pusan. There were over 100 orphanages in the group and each one contained from 60 to 100 children. That came to more than 60,000 children. They were surviving primarily on the assistance they received from KCAC, the Red Cross and the U.S. Army.

I wondered about it. Were all of these children truly orphaned because their parents had been killed in the war, or had many of them simply been abandoned by parents who were still alive. Thousands of these children were less than three years old. The war had been going on longer than that. What kind of man would want to subject his wife to the hardship of being pregnant in the middle of a shooting war? I asked Dr. Chou about it. His answer was, "Who knows? We have children who need to be cared for. We do the best we can."

My Assistant and I, along with the men from my Choir, visited several of the orphanages. We were able to deliver supplies and help coordinate some of the efforts organized by Colonel Slover and Dr. Chou.

As I looked at these little children, in my mind's eye I could not blot out the memory of the little ones running along the railroad tracks in the bitter cold my first night in Korea. I thanked God I was being given the opportunity to do helpful, positive things in the midst of all this devastation and destruction. Many of the men in my unit privately expressed to me that they were glad they were engineers and were building and helping, rather than tearing down. It was a good unit in which to serve.

There was a relatively large number of LDS servicemen stationed among the military units in Pusan. Our Group Leader was a dentist from Phoenix, Arizona named Junius Gibbons. I had met him during the tour with President Robertson the previous month. In my opinion he was a spiritual giant. His counselors were named Heaton and Nash. I was impressed with both of them as well. There was a very nice army chapel located on the Port property in downtown Pusan. The Army Chaplain in charge of this chapel had the responsibility of coordinating its schedule among all the religious groups and denominations who requested the use of it. Somehow the Mormons had the lowest priority on his list. No time could be found when it would be available for them to use.

Gibbons called and asked if I could do anything about it. I visited the Chaplain. Since I was another Army Chaplain he was obligated to make it available any time I requested, so long as it didn't conflict with another Army Chaplain's services. Then my request would rank equally with that other one's and we would have to work it out. We soon had the chapel scheduled for LDS meetings very early Sunday mornings and on Tuesday nights.

As far as the Protestant Services for my own Battalion, I had the small Chapel in the end of our Administration Building within our own compound. I did not need to share it with any other unit. I did need to arrange for my Catholic men to have Mass. There was a Mass held at a unit close by that my men could attend. I was not able to locate a priest to come to my unit specifically to offer

Mass, so I pretty much had the exclusive use of the chapel for my services and Character Guidance lectures. I did manage to locate a Buddhist Priest who could come and hold services for the men of my unit who belonged to that faith.

Christmas was coming, so Wixom and I decided to paint the chapel and make it more presentable. We worked all day. We hadn't quite finished when evening came, but we were getting close. Then we did something stupid, but didn't realize it at the time. We were using gasoline as paint thinner. When we finished we put the paint brushes and the cans of gasoline out on the porch area so they would be ready for use the next day. The next morning we discovered the men who attended the movie the night before had mistaken the cans of gasoline for butt cans. Butt cans are filled with water and placed conveniently so the men may discard their lighted cigarettes as a fire safety precaution. There were several cigarette butts floating in both cans. It had been estimated that if a fire broke out in our old wooden buildings, it would take only about four minutes to level them.

I always thought open flame would ignite gasoline as quickly as an electrical spark would. Evidently that isn't true. If the container is open and the fumes dissipate, the liquid gas does not ignite readily. That was the case here. We never told anyone about it.

One afternoon a dignified Korean lady came to our guard gate and asked for me by name. The Guard called, and I went out to meet her. The Guard was a regular attendee at the chapel. He gave me a knowing look that said, "sooo . . . the chaplain has a girl friend too." I shook my head "no" at him, then turned to meet her.

She had been referred to me by Dr. Chou. She and her husband were located about two blocks away from our compound. Theirs' was not an officially recognized orphanage, but the two of them were taking care of over forty children. They were desperately in need of food, clothing and bedding. The weather was very cold at night.

Wixom and I went to see their circumstances. They were all in one room. They slept on the floor. There was one small stove to keep them warm.

I went to the Mess Hall and asked if there was any food we could spare. The Sergeant told me none of the men would eat Split Pea Soup when he prepared it, and he had a pretty good supply on hand. "Could they use that?" Indeed they could, and did.

We managed to find some old blankets and other food to take to them. I made sure that Gate Guard was one of the men who helped make the delivery so he would not misunderstand the purpose of her visit. Then I called Colonel Slover to see if there was a way this orphanage could be recognized officially so they could get help through his organization. He said he would look into it.

It turned out that there were many forms to fill out and qualifications that must be met. Both the lady and her husband were teachers who held doctors degrees from top name Korean universities. With a few adjustments their operation met the requirements. Actually obtaining the clearance took almost a month. At least the children were receiving the help they needed.

She came again to the compound with another request. Could I help her to teach the children English? She spoke it rather poorly and her husband not at all. I was able to find some unique army hymnals. They had the same hymn repeated on two facing pages. The one on the left page gave it in Korean. The one on the matching right page gave it in English. She had had training so she could read music and teach the children the songs. It seemed to me it would be an ideal instructional tool. I had only two copies of the hymnal, so I gave them to her and ordered twenty more through our supply channels. I was informed, "these hymnals are supposed to be for the use of Army personnel." When I explained to the Chaplain in charge of ecclesiastical supplies why I wanted them, he said they had had quite a few requests from orphanages and other worthy organizations, and did not have sufficient supplies to fill the need. "However, since I am sure you have enough Korean personnel in your Battalion to justify a shipment of ten copies,

I will send them." He knew perfectly well there were no Korean personnel in my Battalion except the houseboys. I was happy he was good hearted and understanding enough to justify sending them and the teaching could be started.

It was very gratifying when some of my Choir men, Wixom and I went to this small orphanage and the children sang several hymns for us phonetically in English.

Chapter 25.

Lt. Sokker Lee

Sokker Lee was a Lieutenant in the Korean Navy who joined the LDS church. One day he called and asked if I could meet with him and a group of his Korean friends who wanted to ask questions about the church. I told him I would be "more than happy to have the opportunity." Little did I realize this was going to be one of the toughest presentations of my life. We met in an old school house. The weather was cold. There were no windows and no source of heat in the building. Present were eleven of the brightest young men I'd ever met. They were all officers in the Korean Navy. We sat down. We were all sort of huddled together, shivering. Brother Lee opened with prayer. Then he indicated I was ready to answer their questions.

Some of them spoke a few words of English. The rest spoke no English at all. Sokker acted as interpreter. His English was very good.

The first question alerted me as to how difficult this discussion was going to be. I was used to dealing with people who had some preconceptions on which to build. These men had almost a completely blank slate with open, inquiring minds.

"What is God?" "I explained that God is 'who', not a 'what'" Sokker translated. "God is the father of our spirits. Every person born into this world is a spirit child of God. He is our Father in Heaven."

"What is Heaven?" This and other such basic questions that most of us take for granted were asked. The men were familiar with the concept of spirits, so we managed to cover that point.

"Who is Jesus Christ?"

"Under the direction of our Heavenly Father, He created the worlds. Then He became the mortal son of our Heavenly Father. He lived His mortal life about two thousand years ago in Jerusalem. He taught us what we should do in order to be able to return to our Heavenly Father and live with Him through all eternity. Evil men put him to death. Three days later He was resurrected. Following that He ascended to Heaven, then came down and appeared to multitudes of people on the American continent."

These were all concepts these men had never heard before. You can imagine the difficulty Sokker and I had explaining them, then translating them into their native language. They were particularly impressed that we believed that all men were brothers and that God loves every one of His children equally. That was when they came up with this haymaker of a question. It was asked with sincerity, not sarcasm.

"If God created the whole earth, and loves all His children the same, why does He give us this horrible war and suffering in our land, and give all good things to America? Why doesn't He treat us all the same?" Most of these young officers had lost parents and other loved ones in the war.

I attempted to explain it from the standpoint of the Plan of Salvation, and the fact that every child of God is given his free agency. Because some men choose to be evil and try to abuse and enslave their fellow men, many suffer from time to time. In regard to America, the Book of Mormon promises that as long as the people who live there live righteously it will be a choice land above all other lands and serve as an example as to how every land could become.

It was a challenge to help them understand the basic tenants of Christian doctrine, even with the use of the Book of Mormon as well as the Bible. They had never been previously exposed to either. I gave them copies of both.

Sokker later told me they had been favorably impressed and several of them were continuing to meet in regular study sessions with him.

Chapter 26.

The Golden Bear

About a week later I received a curious phone call. "Chaplain Beecher? This is the Duty Officer at the Port. We understand you're the top ranking LDS person in this area. They held a major clothing drive in Utah. We have a 100,000 ton ship named The Golden Bear waiting here to be unloaded. How do you intend to handle it?"

This was the first I'd heard of the matter. Wixom and I jumped into the jeep and headed for the Port. There it was . . . a huge ship filled with thousands and thousands of bales of clothing. Indeed, the whole state of Utah had participated in the drive.

I promptly called Colonel Slover. He was delighted.

"Of course I have the people and the means to distribute the clothing to people who need it." Soon he joined us at the port. It didn't take long before his people began unloading the ship.

I asked him if I could have a few bales so I could personally deliver them to some nearby orphanages and refugee camps. "Of course, Chaplain. This is your responsibility. We're merely assisting you. We are accepting these from the people of Utah through you."

Wixom and I loaded several bales into the back of our jeep and headed for our compound. When we got there I couldn't resist going to my commanding officer, Colonel Akins, and sharing my plight with him. "May I have the use of all the vehicles of the Battalion for a few days, to handle the distribution of clothing to people who need it?"

He almost panicked. He came out and looked at the huge bales we had piled on the jeep.

I knew he had previously been involved with a Mormon Chaplain named Covington in a situation that required the use of most of the company's transportation vehicles. It had infringed on the unit's basic mission, but it was for a justifiable cause. Now I was presenting him with an even bigger dilemma. I could see by his face he was a man torn. He had the regular work of the Battalion to accomplish, yet he did not want to refuse his Chaplain's request for help in a humanitarian cause.

I waited and watched him expectantly. "Uh . . . Chappie . . . couldn't you use just four or five trucks from Headquarters Company for a few days?"

"Colonel, you've got to come down to the port and see for yourself. It's a huge ship!" He just stood there shaking his head. Finally he said, "Aren't there some other units nearby who could help us. Is the whole thing your responsibility?"

Finally I couldn't hold it back any longer. "Colonel, I knew you'd come through for me. I have to confess, I've already called Colonel Slover of KCAC. They're taking care of the whole thing." He looked relieved. Then he turned and looked at me. "You put me through all this as a joke?" "I'm sorry, sir. I just couldn't resist it. I knew how I felt when I first learned about it, and I wanted to share those feelings with you. I do have one small request. Can I take some of the men from the Choir with me to deliver the clothes from these bales to some nearby refugee camps?"

He was smiling now. "Take whatever you want, Chappie. Just let the Adjutant know what's going on. Tell Captain Glover of Headquarters Company that I said you can use whatever vehicles you need to haul the men wherever you want to go. Also tell him you have my permission to take whichever men you request to go with you."

On two or three occasions we took ten men and four jeeps. Some were from the LDS Group, most were from my Protestant Choir. We drove to several of the refugee camps that were located on the outskirts of Pusan. There we cut open the burlap protection and began handing out the clothing to the people who crowded around our vehicles.

A couple of memories stand out most vividly. At the Bum Il Dong camp, there was a very wrinkled, toothless old Mama-son. We found a heavy winter woolen coat that looked like it would fit her. One of our men assisted her in trying it on. Her face lit up with a smile that was one of my favorite photographs of the war.

The Camp Director had a three year old daughter that could only be described as "a living doll." Her black hair was cut in a style that we Westerners would call the "Dutch Boy." It was very straight, parted in the middle, with bangs cut straight across her forehead. She was a beautiful child. Wixom found a red coat with a fur collar that was just her size.

There were several other touching moments as we handed out those clothes. I noticed several of our men had tears in their eyes because they were so moved by the experience.

We sent several pictures to the Deseret News so the folks back home in Utah could see the good that was resulting from their generosity. It turned out that during the clothing drive the publicity had centered on a little blond girl with a Shirley Temple hairstyle. She was pictured donating a red coat with a fur collar. The newspaper ran the pictures of the little blond donor and the little Korean recipient side by side. These two beautiful children from the Western and Eastern hemispheres seemed to represent the whole world.

It could have been the same coat. We had no knowledge of the drive before the ship arrived. We had not seen any of the publicity. We didn't know which bale would contain such a coat. But, what a fortunate choice of pictures to send back to the newspaper. The News editor wrote me a letter that said it was one of the best things to come out of the war. The effect of those pictures on the people back home was "electrifying!"

Again I thanked my Heavenly Father that I could participate in constructive, helpful things in the middle of such destruction. Many of the other fellows' testimonies in subsequent Testimony Meetings were fervent and filled with similar gratitude.

Chapter 27.

A Painting Of The Savior

Another thing that stands out in my memory of Korea is the lack of the color green. Everything was dusty brown or gray. The people dressed primarily in white, and sometimes black. The men liked to wear a particular style of funny black hats. Most of the green plants that you would expect to see on the mountain sides or along the highways had been destroyed in battle or burned during the winter as the people attempted to survive the cold weather. By its absence, I came to appreciate what a beautiful color green is.

In the window of an artist's shop about half way up the hill on the road between my unit and the main supply route, there was a picture about two feet wide and three feet high that showed Christ with three children in a lush green garden. The picture centered on a girl about five or six years old who was sitting on His lap. A girl about twelve years old stands nearby. A nine or ten year old boy is sitting at His feet holding a toy airplane. The expression on the Savior's face as He talks to the children is loving and caring. I wanted that picture.

I went into the shop. The artist explained, "It is copy of famous painting by American artist, Harry Anderson. It title, 'What Happened To Your Hand?' Little girl asking." The price was $65.00. That was more than I had at that time. Unknown to me, Wixom talked to the men in my choir. They chipped in and bought it for me and autographed it on the back. It is difficult to convey how pleased and grateful to them I felt.

It did not have the artist's signature. I asked him to sign it for me. He refused. "It not original. It copy. I not get good paints because of war. It calcimine. Not my good work." I could not persuade him to sign it. I've forgotten his name.

We hung it in the front of the battalion chapel for several weeks. Many of the men expressed appreciation for the message it conveyed. It added a special feeling during our meetings. The resurrected Savior has quite a story to tell about what happened to His hands.

As the time approached for me to begin thinking about rotating home, I wrote to my wife and said I was sending her a large wonderful picture of the Savior that we "could hang above our mantle in our own little home, when we get it." It was a couple of years later that she confided her initial reaction when I first wrote her about it. She was worried that it would be one of those overly sanctimonious pictures of Him. "When I saw the actual picture, I was delighted. You hadn't gone off the deep end after all."

That picture remains one of our most prized possessions.

Chapter 28.

Gibbons and Cohen - A Conversion!

Someone once said, "Dentists and lawyers run the church." Our LDS Group Leader in Pusan was a dentist from Phoenix Arizona named Junius Gibbons. I had previously met him during President Robertson's tour. He'd had a friend of the Jewish persuasion with him named Irving Cohen who was also a dentist. Junius and Irving attended several testimony meetings where the Spirit was present.

After considerable coaxing Junius persuaded Irving to read the Book of Mormon. Irving said he'd enjoyed it but was not convinced of its divine authenticity. Junius pointed out Moroni's promise in the 10th chapter and asked Irving to pray about it. Irving complied. No result.

"Did you pray in the name of Christ, the way it says?"

"Of course not. You can't expect me to pray in Christ's name. I'm Jewish!"

"Well, that's what it says you have to do. It won't hurt to try."

Again, considerable coaxing. Irving finally prayed and reluctantly asked in the name of Christ. His prayer was answered in a way he did not expect.

He reported that he was not asleep and definitely was not dreaming. His room began to fill with light. The Book of Mormon that lay on the table beside his bed was glowing. A personage of light descended into his room, pointed toward the Book and nodded "yes."

Irving was overwhelmed. It took him almost three days to recover. He had not expected such a literal answer to his prayer. When he told some of his friends about it, they thought he'd had a nervous breakdown.

Junius asked him when he was going to be baptized.

"I can't do that. My wife would leave me. My family would bury me . . . literally. That's what they do when you leave the Jewish faith."

"Can you just ignore what happened?"

"No."

"Well, what are you going to do about it?"

"What can I do about it?"

"Why don't you pray and ask if you should be baptized?"

It took a few weeks to work up the courage, but eventually he did. That night a storm arose. Water leaked in the window and collected under his bed so that he had to step into it to get out of bed. He had stayed in that same room for over six months. There had been several storms, and this was the first time it had leaked in this manner.

"Is that good enough for you?"

"It could be coincidence."

"Yes, it could. Do you think it was?"

Irving was taking no chances. The next night he moved his bed to the other end of the room. He prayed. That night another storm arose. This time the window leaked in such a way that the water collected in the other end of the room from where it had been the night before. Again he had to step into water to get out of bed.

"Another coincidence?"

"No. I'm convinced. My prayers have been answered. But how can I take such a step without clearing it with my wife and family? I'm sure they'd never approve."

"Get them to read the Book of Mormon."

"You have no idea what a challenge that would be."

Later that week Irving received a letter from his wife. In it she described a dream she'd had where he returned home from the army, then they drove thousands of miles to get married. She raised the question, "Why would we do that when we're already married?" Junius had already explained Temple Marriage to him. Irving considered this an additional sign that he was to join the church. He had Junius baptize him. Irving notified his wife and family. They did not receive the message well.

It was about this time that my unit moved to Pusan and I learned the story about Irving's vision and subsequent baptism. When I heard that Irving was a literal descendent of Aaron, and that he had his personal genealogy back to Aaron himself, I thought, "this man could become the means of fulfilling the prophecy in the 14th Section of the D&C. He's going to be an important person to watch."

About a week or so later I was visiting Junius in his office when he suddenly bent over in pain. He had a lump in his right side about the size of a tennis ball. I felt it. I walked him to his dispensary. When I called the next day he told me the lump had disappeared and he was feeling well. The doctors couldn't explain it.

Meanwhile, Irving disappeared or rather was transferred unexpectedly. In his capacity as one of Irving's friends, Junius called his unit to get information concerning as to where he had been transferred. He was given no information whatever. He suggested that I call, in my official capacity as Irving's Chaplain, and see if I could have more success. I called. I learned he'd been sent to a Depot that was only a temporary holding station which kept no track of where people went from there. No one in his previous unit could give us any information.

The long awaited day of the end of my tour of duty in Korea arrived. This was to be my last Sunday meeting with my brethren. I was to begin my trip home that night. Orders had been cut for me to go to Yong Dong Po to board a ship and head stateside. Whoopee!

That morning I went to Priesthood Meeting at the Port Chapel. Junius was not there. His counselor, Brother Nash, conducted the meeting. We called Junius' unit. They said he was in the hospital. The lump in his side had returned.

There were twenty-three elders in attendance at that meeting. We went as a single body to visit him in the hospital.

The nurse came into the room. "Only two visitors are permitted at one time."

I answered her, "We're not just visitors. We're clergy. All of us. Do you have any olive oil?" She looked at the cross on my collar and decided not to give us any argument. Shortly she returned with a small bottle of oil. We consecrated it. Then all twenty three of us participated in administering a blessing to Junius. Nash annointed, I sealed.

I remember the Spirit directed me to tell him he would be completely healed within twenty-four hours, and would never be bothered with this ailment again.

Later that night, on the train to Yong Dong Po, I thought about what I had said in that blessing. That's a mighty strong promise to give someone.

Junius's other counselor, Grant Heaton, was on that same train. He was also going home, but his situation was different from mine. He had completed his time in the military service and was about to receive his discharge. I still had fourteen more months to go.

He was either expecting to be called or had already been called to become the first Mission President in the South East Asia area in Hong Kong. I was impressed with his capability. He spoke Chinese fluently. He was an outstanding young man. I said to myself, "I'm probably looking at a future General Authority." Our conversation lasted most of the night.

Next day, at the Replacement Depot, I phoned Nash in Pusan to get the latest news about Junius' condition. He said he'd gone to the hospital and learned that Junius was no longer there. He'd called his unit, and he wasn't there either. He didn't know where he was.

I called the hospital and asked about him. I was told he'd been sent to the Hospital Ship. That was all they would tell me. The Spirit had been so strong during the blessing, yet apparently he'd taken a turn for the worst.

I was left to wonder about it until three years later when I was back in civilian life and living in California. One Sunday morning both Gibbons and Cohen showed up at a Sacrament meeting I was attending. I asked them what happened? Where were they? I wanted to hear the end of the story. Here it is.

Gibbons told me the lump in his side reappeared as a dark mass on his X-ray. The next morning a new X-ray showed absolutely nothing. It had completely disappeared. The doctors couldn't explain it. They decided to send him to more advanced medical facilities to see if it could be understood what was going on. They sent him to the Hospital Ship, which in turn sent him to the largest, most advanced medical facility in Tokyo. No one could find anything wrong with him, nor could they deny what the X-rays showed.

Meanwhile he was feeling fine, so he was bored. He began wandering around the hospital. He happened to go past a locked Psychiatric Ward and look in. There was Cohen!

Cohen was overjoyed to see him. "Thank God! I've been praying you'd be sent to me."

Cohen explained that after he'd been baptized, the Jewish Welfare Board in New York heard from his family that he'd seen a vision and deserted the faith. It had inquired about it through medical channels. He had been brought to this facility in Tokyo and questioned extensively by the doctors in an effort to find the cause of his personality disorder. "The only thing they can find wrong with me is I said I've seen a vision. I don't know how long they intend to keep me here."

Gibbons promptly called Chaplain Madsen who was stationed in Tokyo at that time. Chaplain Madsen knew some of the doctors personally. He called for an appointment which I was told went something like this:

"I understand you've been holding one of our church members under psychiatric observation for weeks. Why"

"He said he's seen an angel or a vision of some sort."

"What's wrong with that?"

"He's suffering from dilusions."

"How long do you intend to hold him?"

"Until we get to the bottom of what's bothering him."

"The best way you can do that is to read the Book of Mormon, pray about it, and receive your own personal understanding."

"That isn't an alternative."

"Then let me suggest another.

I know someone in Washington, D.C. who will be very interested in your lengthy interrogation. His name is Ezra Taft Benson. He's the Secretary of Agriculture in President Eisenhower's Cabinet. He's also an Apostle in our Church. I intend to call him. I guarantee he will personally and promptly look into this situation. You see, in our church we believe in visions and angels and personal revelation from God in answer to prayer."

The call to Washington was not necessary. The doctors started the paperwork that afternoon and released Cohen the next morning. They realized that what they were doing was a form of religious persecution that could rapidly develop into a political "hot potato" that they weren't prepared to handle.

Cohen later told me, "that experience made me understand in my own small way what Joseph Smith had to endure."

There was one other important detail I tried to take care of before I left Korea. I had a long conversation with Captain Glover, Headquarters Company commander, about getting Wixom promoted. I told him that Wixom was the best heavy equipment operator and the most reliable man in the battalion. He wouldn't believe me. "If he's so good, Chappie, why is he assigned to you? . . . so you can keep an eye on him?"

"That's not the way it is at all, sir. He watches after me."

He wasn't convinced. I left Korea feeling disappointed because this matter was not concluded satisfactorily.

Chapter 29.

The Trip Home / U.S.S. Serpent / Easter Sunday

The trip home from Korea was not pleasant. I had always imagined an ocean voyage would be exciting and exotic. It wasn't. Something unexpected happened. I got seasick. Never before (except for Deardon and his airplane antics) had I suffered from motion sickness. As a child I would often lie in the back seat of my parents' car reading comic books with my head toward the floor and feet propped up in the window and I would not get sick.

The trip across the Pacific Ocean was aboard the U.S.S. Serpent. It was a round-bottomed vessel that took an interminably long time to roll slowly from one side to the other, then back again. The army was in such a hurry to get me to Korea that it flew me there. It was in no hurry to get me home. It took sixteen days.

I would take Dramamine, lie in my bunk and "let it roll." My stomach kept rolling with it. Five other men shared the same tight quarters. There were usually at least three of us lying in our bunks. Many times we were lying there during mealtimes. Food was of little interest.

I recall one morning an orderly came in and insisted I get off my bunk so he could make it up. One of the other men had already thrown up and the orderly had cleaned it away. The smell lingered and made most of us even more sick than we already were. About the third time he suggested I get up I said simply, "If I get vertical, you'll have another mess to clean up." He promptly replied, "Just stay horizontal, sir. I hope you feel better soon."

The second day out they published a duty roster. It called for me to be the Officer Of The Day. I wasn't sure what that meant on shipboard, so I reported in to find out. When the officer in charge saw me he exclaimed, "You're a Chaplain!"

"That's right, sir."

"You can't be the officer of the day. Sorry for the inconvenience, Chaplain." He called for his clerk. They had to completely re-do and re-post the roster throughout the whole ship. I spent some time with him that morning while he explained some of the features of the ship and acquainted me with sea lore.

Easter came. The sea rolled gently. Chaplain Wood of the Afro-Methodist church and I scheduled six Easter Services, one for each deck's personnel. I presented the sermon for three of them and played the organ for the other three when Chaplain Wood preached. He played the organ when I preached. The ship's chapel was on F-deck. It was at the lowest level. It was hot with poor ventilation.

Chaplain Wood gave the first sermon. I sat at the organ, listening and wondering how long it would be before I threw-up on the keyboard. Should I make a run for the latrine and disrupt his service, or sit there and contain myself? I decided to sit there. I remember looking down at the two keyboards and foot pedals. Suddenly the scene from the movie "A Song To Remember" flashed into my mind. Cornel Wilde (as Chopin) was playing a concert. He coughed up blood. A spot of it appeared on the keys. I said to myself, "I hope I don't make a bigger mess than that on this keyboard." Then I kept repeating to myself, "Don't think about it, don't think about it" as I tried to concentrate on what the Chaplain was saying in his sermon. That service ran the longest twenty-five minutes of my life.

When he concluded we both went up on the deck and gasped fresh air. He looked at me and said, "Five more to go." I asked him if he felt as queasy as I did. He did.

I gave the next sermon. Somehow standing at the pulpit and speaking to the group, (we had about 25 to 45 men come to each service), did not seem as hot and confining as sitting in the stuffy, tight alcove where the organ was located. At the organ you felt closed in, unable to breath because of the lack of oxygen and hotness of the air.

We went to the deck the second time. Chaplain Wood observed, "It's even worse at the organ."

"You're right."

"Well, it's my turn to speak. See that you don't disturb my sermon by making any sudden exits."

"You'd rather I stay and . . . ?"

"No! Leave if you have to. But only if you have to." We both laughed and went inside.

After the final sermon had been delivered with no mishaps, we went back up on deck. There were many young men standing nearby admiring the sunset. "Maybe that's why so many of us stay up here in the open air most of the time." We stayed for a while and quietly expressed our gratitude to our Heavenly Father because the voyage was a relatively calm one, and we were safely going home . . . home from a war. That was the truly Easter moment.

At long last the voyage ended in Seattle. I caught an airplane home to Salt Lake City. I caught a cab to Aunt Blanche's house where Marguerite was staying. It was after 10:00 p.m. when I arrived. I remember standing on the front porch and ringing the doorbell. I waited in anticipation for her to answer the door. When she opened it she had just finished washing her hair. It was wonderful to see her again.

Section 4 :

Stateside

Chapter 30.

Fort Huachuca, Arizona

After a few days leave I was assigned to report to Fort Huachuca, Arizona. Marguerite and I packed our belongings in our little blue Plymouth and headed South. It was with a feeling of great happiness and freedom mixed with anticipation that we finally began our married life together, knowing that this time we could enjoy being together without the threat of imminent separation hanging over our heads.

Fort Huachuca was a beautiful place. The fame of the Arizona sunsets is well deserved. "Huachuca" means "thunder in the mountains." It is well named. You can almost set your watch by the timing of the gentle rain during the rainy season.

We were assigned a small free-standing house. It had a kitchen, living room, bedroom, and a covered porch that could serve as an extra bedroom when company came.

Chaplain White was the Post Chaplain. He was from the Disciples of Christ Church. His family lived about two blocks away from us. He assigned me to Chapel E which was located geographically near the center of the Post.

I was assigned to one Communications unit, but was expected to serve several surrounding units in such a way that my actual unit assignment became somewhat secondary to coordinating my work through the Post Chaplain's office.

Chaplain White was a delight to work with. He and Chaplain Wylie (Methodist) and I would trade off giving services in each other's chapels. That way we each worked with all the men at all the chapels on the post. Chaplain Wylie had the assignment to cover services for men in the Stockade. I covered the services in the Hospital.

Marguerite was pregnant. She suffered from morning sickness. I could appreciate what she was going through because her nausea reminded me of my own seasickness during my trip home. Mine lasted only sixteen days, hers went on for months. She was wonderful about it. She never complained.

Marguerite began playing the organ for my Sunday Services. It was at the end of my first month on the Post that Chaplain White scheduled me to give the sermon at the Post Chapel the next Sunday. The choir rehearsed on Thursday nights. Marguerite was having a particularly bad evening so I volunteered to play the organ.

There were about thirty people in the choir. The volunteer director was Colonel Baker, the Provost Marshall on the post. He looked at the hymnal, then announced, "Chaplain White didn't give me the songs we're supposed to sing. Has anyone seen him?" I spoke up. "He's going to be away this weekend. He's speaking at one of the churches in Bisbee."

"Does anyone know what the subject of the sermon will be?"

I suggested a couple of hymns that would be appropriate. The Colonel looked at me. "Did he give you a list?"

"No. I chose them myself."

"Did you check with the Chaplain?"

"Yes, sir. These are the ones I want."

He looked at me as if I was overstepping my authority. Then he saw the cross on my collar. "You're the new Chaplain?"

"That's right."

"How come you're playing the organ?"

"Oh. My wife's supposed to play, but she's not feeling well tonight, so I'm filling in. She'll be playing on Sunday. She's a lot better at it than I am."

The rehearsal went well. We all became good friends. His friendship was to become especially important when I was assigned supervision over the Teen-Age Club a couple of months later.

It was about my third week on the post that I received a phone call at 2:00 a.m. from the Hospital. "Chaplain, there's been a bad automobile accident. One of the men is asking for you."

There were five young black soldiers returning to the Post after a night of drinking in a nearby town. The car had missed a turn at high speed and rolled over several times. Four of the men were dead before help arrived. The fifth man had asked for the Chaplain. He was a powerful athlete about 6'4" tall, 240 pounds and twenty one years of age. He had everything to live for.

"Chaplain, I can't move. I can't feel my hands and feet. Can you help me? I'm freezing. Can you get me a couple more blankets? Are my friends all right?" He started to cry. "I saw some ambulances taking them away. They looked like they were all dead."

I did what I could to comfort him. I told him we would get in touch with his parents and fiancée. He gave me their names, addresses and phone numbers. I wrote them down. Again he complained of being cold. I stepped into the hall, found an orderly and asked him to bring a couple of blankets. The room didn't seem cold to me. I figured the young man was in shock.

I returned to the patient. He talked about home, his plans when he got out of the army. He talked about his fiancée' and their wedding plans. He shared his doubt and fears. I spent an hour listening and comforting him as best I could. He complained of still feeling cold. I said I would see if I could get the orderly to bring some more blankets or a heating pad.

As I stepped into the hall again his doctor was approaching. "Doctor, he's still feeling cold. Can we get him a heating pad?"

"It won't help, Chaplain. He will feel cold no matter what we do. His spinal chord is severed. He won't live through the night."

I offered a silent prayer, composed myself and returned to his room. I told him the orderly was getting some more blankets. I prayed vocally with him, and comforted him the best I could, then encouraged him to get some sleep. I sat with him another hour . . . until he passed away.

I said to myself, "Dear God, is this assignment going to be another one like Camp Cooke? Am I going to have to face something like this every weekend?" I lost more men from my unit at Camp Cooke in six months due to traffic accidents than in fourteen months of war in Korea. It is not one of my favorite tasks to tell wives, children, parents, brothers and sisters or sweethearts that someone they love has been killed.

Alcohol played a significant roll in the majority of the deaths I had to deal with. I hate it with a passion.

Chapter 31.

Butch

Marguerite spent a lot of time alone in our little house. We were both excited about our coming blessed event. Both of us had been "only children" so we'd had no experience dealing with babies or siblings.

We got some training from an unexpected source that could be loosely compared to raising a child. Chaplain White's Springer Spaniel had puppies. His wife sold or gave all of them away except one. He was a beautiful little dog, the pick of the litter. Marguerite was visiting with Mrs. White one day and that last puppy came to her. She picked him up and held him on her lap. It was love at first sight. We bought him.

The White children had named him "Storm King" in honor of the frequent, timely storms at the fort. We called him "Butch." Butch grew rapidly. He was bright. It didn't take him long to become house broken. He was inquisitive, into everything, and active. He could go from one thing to the next quicker than you could clean it up.

He was great company. He never saw anyone he didn't like. He would follow almost anyone anywhere. It kept us busy tracking him down and retrieving him from his latest adventure. Fortunately the area of the post where we lived was a tight-knit community. Everybody knew "the Chaplain's dog" and was helpful in looking after him.

One morning he followed a neighbor's child to school. I went to the schoolyard to get him. It took me almost ten minutes to catch him. He was happily racing from one youngster to the next and basking in the affection they gave him. To my amazement, every child in the whole school knew him by name. Finally one youngster grabbed him and carried him over to me. It was almost funny but it could have been serious. He had his arm around Butch's neck and was holding him by his head. Butch's body was swinging like a pendulum. I grabbed the choking puppy and thanked the helpful child. As I carried him off the school ground Butch struggled and whined because he wanted to go back and play some more.

Marguerite is an accomplished pianist. We obtained a small Spinet and put it in our living room. One of my favorite pieces she played was the Liszt Concert Etude in D Flat. I decided to learn it. Evidently it was Butch's favorite piece. Whenever either one of us was playing the piano he would ignore us except when we played that particular piece. When we started it he would come running and lie at our feet by the piano. When we reached a certain run that begins in the high register and goes almost the full length of the keyboard, he would howl! The first time he did it, it sounded like something unearthly. I thought something was wrong and stopped to see what was affecting him. He seemed fine. Then I went back to practicing. I repeated the run. He howled. I soon learned that he howled every time that run was played, and that was the only time he howled. Evidently there was something harmonically present in that run that made him want to sing to it.

Butch took up a lot of our time. He was good company for Marguerite when I was away from home. One night I was just completing an evening service when the phone rang. My assistant said it was Marguerite. "She sounds like she's beside herself. It's an emergency."

"You've got to come home right now! Butch was chasing a skunk and got himself sprayed. I made him come in, but he smelled so strong I sent him back out. He started chasing the skunk again. He's been sprayed four times!"

I hurriedly wrapped up my business at the chapel and drove home. The whole neighborhood was fragrant.

It took a few minutes to catch him. It was tricky to get hold of him yet not get the smell on my clothes. I finally tied a leash on him. He smelled so bad we couldn't take him in the house. I felt guilty leaving him outside that cold February night, but I had no choice. Besides, it might teach him a lesson. He whined a couple of hours then settled into his dog house.

The next morning I went outside. He was as frisky and happy as ever and showed no signs of being uncomfortable because of the weather. Amazingly, he had no odor on him. I took him to the veterinarian so he could de-odorize him. The Vet looked him over and said, "I can't smell anything."

"He got sprayed four times. The whole neighborhood still reeks of it."

"Maybe when he's wet it will bring it out. He gave Butch a bath in tomato juice and washed it off. I assisted. If there's anything Butch hated, it was a bath. Both the Vet and I were splashed with suds and partially soaked before we were through. There was no odor on Butch. We talked it over and tried to find an explanation as to how he managed to eliminate the odor entirely before morning. We found no solution to the mystery. On the other hand, it took a couple of weeks for our house to get rid of the skunk smell that had been introduced by Butch's brief visit when she called him in after the first time he'd been sprayed.

Donald Bailey was my assistant. He was married to a beautiful young lady named Mildred who'd served in the same mission field that I had served in. She was an outstanding Lady Missionary. We were proud to have them living in a mobile home close by us. They had a daughter just over a year old. The baby loved Butch.

We were impressed by how careful he was around her. He seemed to understand she was a baby and not able to play as roughly as the school kids were.

One night Don, Mildred and the baby were visiting us. We adults were busy talking and not paying close attention to what Butch and the baby were doing. Suddenly I noticed she had a balloon in her hand. It was not inflated. She was sticking her arm down Butch's throat. His choking sound caught my attention. I was afraid he might bite her, or at least growl or bark and scare her. To my amazement, he simply got free, stood up, walked away and lay down about six feet from her.

She followed, tripped on his paws and fell so that she sat down hard right on top of him. It looked like it knocked the wind out of him. Without making a sound he moved again. She followed, stepped on his legs and sat down on him again. She began trying to put the balloon in his mouth and her fingers in his eyes. He got away and moved again. She followed.

He moved again, only this time he came over, put his head in my wife's lap, looked up at her and whined. He'd had enough. He was clearly pleading "Call her off!" I was proud of him. Don picked up his daughter and held her in his lap after that. She squirmed and cried, but he wouldn't let her go. They had to cut their visit short because of her fussing. She and Butch remained good friends for the remainder of the time we were stationed at the Fort.

One day Marguerite said to me, "I'm sure he's getting up on the furniture, although he knows he's not allowed to."

"What makes you think that?"

"I keep finding dog hair on the couch and chairs, although I've never seen him on them."

"Let's go outside and peek through the window to see what he does."

It was one of the funniest moments I can remember. We went outside the house so Marguerite could look in one of the windows. I had to lift her up on my shoulders because our house was on a hill and the windows were fairly high above the ground on the outside. When she looked in, Butch was standing with his front paws on the back of the couch looking out. Their noses almost touched. She let out a shout and twitched so that I almost dropped her. Butch realized he was caught, and took off. We rushed back into the house. It took a while, but we finally found him hiding under the bed.

One afternoon I came out of my chapel. It was raining as usual that hour. I saw a very pregnant young lady and a dog running across the parade field toward me. I realized it was my wife and dog. It is strange how certain brief images stick in your mind. This was one of the most beautiful sights I've ever seen.

On another occasion I looked out of my office window. I saw men running back and forth in a disorganized manner. I stepped out of the front door to see what was going on.

"Head him off."

"No, he's coming your way."

Soon I realized there was a recreational baseball game being played on the field behind my chapel. Somehow, Butch had left my office without my realizing it. He'd run onto the field, grabbed the ball, and had both teams running in all directions trying to catch him. He loved the attention.

The minute I stepped out of the chapel door he came running up to me and gave me the ball. "Is this what you're looking for, gentlemen?"

"We thought it was your dog, Chaplain. We've been chasing him for five minutes. Could you please keep him inside?"

"I'll be glad to. They resumed their game. Butch went to the window. He kept jumping up to see what was going on outside. He made such a fuss I finally gave up trying to get anything accomplished and took him home.

Chapter 32.

Character Guidance Lectures

Character Guidance lectures were required to be given on the Post. Basically the manual was well written, but it is hard to deliver good solid uplifting rah, rah material that has been entirely created by someone else. Many chaplains resort to reading them which is a deadly way of delivery. The lectures primarily conveyed messages of keeping your morals high, being proud to be an American, especially an American service man, and so forth. It was a captive audience. It was not in a church setting. Individual motivation and endorsement were lacking. The men generally regarded these sessions as boring and somewhat demeaning.

Most of the lectures were scheduled for the period right after lunch. To eat, then go into a darkened theater and listen to someone read out of a manual was an invitation to take a nap. The men took advantage of it.

I was searching for ways to make the lectures enjoyable, stimulating, less obligatory, yet still get the point across. The subject of my next scheduled lecture was "drinking." I thought, "I can stand there and relate all the bad things about alcohol, and bore everyone to death, or . . . " I got an idea. There was a Sergeant

Major who was well known on the post for getting drunk. I asked if he'd be willing to work on a skit with me.

"Here's the plot. I go on stage and begin reading the lecture on alcohol in a hum drum voice. About two minutes into it everybody will be turned off and falling asleep. I want you to make a big disturbance off stage that will wake them up and get their attention. Then you stagger on stage and disrupt my presentation. I'll leave in dismay. Several young soldiers will follow you onto stage and you offer them each a swig of the "big orange". You'll wind up getting drunk on stage together. We'll work out some details about what you'll talk about . . . who had an accident, who got court marshaled, who had this problem and who had that problem. Then after you've cleverly made the points outlined in the lesson manual, I'll come back on stage and conclude the session."

"I'd like to help you, Chaplain, but . . . " He didn't feel comfortable. It took lengthy convincing to talk him into it. We chose four young recruits and held a couple of secret rehearsals.

The day for the presentation came. The men arrived in the semi-darkened theater. Everyone was sleepy. I went on stage and began to drone my lecture. Suddenly a flat board about twelve feet long fell and smacked loudly against the floor. A rifle shot would not have generated more attention. The Sergeant's drunken baritone was heard off stage. I struggled valiantly to ignore what was going on and continue my lecture. He staggered on stage with a bottle in one hand and a cup in the other. He took a long drink from the bottle.

I saw his Commanding Officer jump out of his seat on the back row and begin running down the aisle on the double. Quickly I closed my book and left the stage. From the wings I kept an eye on the Captain. He slowed down indecisively and stopped at about the fourth row. He wasn't sure if this was a put-on or the genuine thing. There was electricity in the air. Everyone was wide awake. Everybody knew the Sergeant and the Captain.

The four recruits came on stage. The Sarge offered them the "Big Orange." They pulled off their skit beautifully.

I reentered the stage and thanked them by name for helping make this lecture more enjoyable. They were all instantly sober. They bowed to the audience and exited amid applause. That's the first time I can remember the men applauding one of my character guidance lectures.

After it was over, I was thanking the Sergeant and congratulating him on being such a good sport. He said, "Chaplain, when I saw my Captain coming down that aisle, I almost had heart failure. I could see my whole career of over twenty years going down the tubes. When you left the stage, I got really desperate."

"Well, Sarge. It didn't show. You were terrific. You looked drunk and feeling no pain, no matter what."

By then the Captain joined us. "Chaplain, the next time you pull something like this, you let me know. I was ready to have the Sarge drawn and quartered. His stripes were history."

"Captain, whether you know it or not, your participation is what made it all come alive. If you'd known about it, it wouldn't have been half as effective. This way everyone got the message."

For the next week or so the Sarge and his Captain were the "toast of the post." Everyone was talking about them. Chaplain White quietly commented about my unorthodox methods for giving character guidance lectures. Then he broke into a smile and said "Wish I'd thought of it. How'd you talk the Sarge into it"

"It wasn't easy," I replied.

About two weeks later I was scheduled to give the Post Headquarters Company a similar after-lunch lecture. When we arrived the theater was locked up. There were some workmen painting the front of the building. I asked them to remove the pins from the door hinges so we could go in. They did. We did. The lecture turned out okay, but not as much fun as the previous one had been.

The Special Services Officer for the post, a Major by rank, was outraged that I had broken into his theater. He cornered Chaplain White and me in the Post Chaplain's office and read us the riot act. "How dare you show everyone in the world how easy it is to break into our building!"

I tried to explain that it didn't take a nuclear physicist to see that anyone could remove pins from door hinges. He said he was considering having me court marshaled for breaking and entering. I defended myself. "I was only following orders. The General made it clear he wants those lectures given."

At that point he gave both me and Chaplain White (who held the same rank as he did) a direct order that "If that building is locked, you dismiss the men and send them back to their units! Is that clear?" We both said "Yes, sir."

The next week I was scheduled for another lecture in the theater. When we got there it was locked. I dismissed the 250 men and sent them back to their unit. Their commanding officer wanted to know why we didn't just "call someone, or get a key, or take the doors off the hinges, and go in." I explained to him that I had received a direct order from the Special Services Officer to dismiss the men if the building wasn't ready. He was angry about my not holding the lecture.

The General heard about it (not from me). The very next day the Special Services Officer was transferred to Korea. I never saw him again. After that the building was well prepared, and on time for all activities scheduled in it.

Chapter 33.

The Post Teen-Age Club

One afternoon I got a phone call from Chaplain White asking me to come to his office. It was an unusual time of the week for him to call, so I was wondering what was going on.

He explained. The Post had a club for teen-age dependents of military personnel. These were not members of the Army themselves, but were the civilian children who lived on post. "There has been a crisis at the club. All the key people on the post had a meeting this afternoon to see how we can resolve it. I told them that the Latter-day Saint Church had an outstanding program for young people and that you were expert at it. We've decided to turn the operation of the club over to you. You'll have the complete cooperation and back-up of the Post Command, and you can give us guidance as to what you need. What do you need?"

What did I need?! I was floored. I'd known that the big three-story building near the center of the post was a club of some kind, but that was all I knew about it. "What kind of problems have they been having?"

"Oh, various and sundry. You know, the kinds of things young people get into when they aren't subject to military discipline."

"In the church the M.I.A. is an organization that encompasses the Boy Scouts program and equivalent things for girls."

"Yes. That's what we want."

"I didn't even make tenderfoot."

"Didn't you tell me you were a Counselor in the Presidency?"

"Yes. But that was when I was older."

"See, you know all about it. You'll do just fine. Here's a roster of the parents who've been participating in the program. Feel free to call on any of them anytime you need help." I left his office feeling overwhelmed.

The parents had been taking turns chaperoning the club. Two couples were there each night of the week. I decided to take Wednesday nights all by myself to get to know the young people.

The second floor of the building was a huge gymnasium. It had basketball hoops and a stage. It was similar to the Cultural Hall of my Ward back home. There was a juke box you could play for free. It had a good selection of current hits on it. Maybe my Arthur Murray teaching experience could come in handy. I decided to try teaching dancing to the young people.

Most of the youngsters were a delight to work with. We quickly became friends. My second week some of them came and said there were "people downstairs in the kitchen, making a mess." I went down to check on it. No one was there . . . just the mess. Several of them came along and helped. We had it cleaned up in about twenty minutes, then we went upstairs. I knew they knew who had made it, but they weren't going to tell on each other.

I asked the friendly ones to patrol the building and help me keep an eye out for potential trouble. They did. They were more effective than having four parents patrolling the place.

About my third week one young man kept interrupting the rest of us in what we were trying to do. I asked him what was his problem. He told me that what I was doing was "stupid and boring. Why don't you do something fun?"

"The others are enjoying it. I'm sure you will too, if you join in. Meanwhile, if you don't like it and can't suggest something positive, please don't interrupt."

He replied, "That's what they said last night."

I'd heard there had been a problem the night before, so this began to explain it. "Who said?"

"That stupid Major and his wife. They even told me to go home."

"Why would they do that?"

"Look, I chew up Majors and spit them out. You're nothing but a crummy Lieutenant, so don't play games with me!"

"I wouldn't think of it. What's your name, again?"

"I'm Colonel So-and-so's son!"

"Oh, I know your father. He's a very nice man."

He looked surprised. "You know my Dad? How'd you get to know him?"

"I shake his hand when I give the service at the Post Chapel. In fact, I'm scheduled to be there next Sunday. I'll make you a deal. If you cause any more trouble, I'll tell him about it on Sunday morning. And if I don't get a chance to tell him privately at the door, I'll do it over the pulpit in front of God and the General and everybody on Post. Okay?"

He was stunned. "You wouldn't!"

"Try me. I give you my word of honor as a Chaplain. I would."

"That's blackmail!"

"I'm glad you thought of it."

The other young people were a ways off, but they heard enough to get the drift of our conversation. One of the most attractive young ladies was the daughter of the couple he had had the run-in with the night before. She came over and asked him to dance. Reluctantly at first he agreed. Gradually he joined in and finally began to enjoy himself.

The next Sunday when he and his father arrived at the Post Chapel, I shook their hands and greeted him warmly by name.

His look of apprehension was replaced by a smile. He became one of my most reliable helpers at the club.

Not all of my problems at the club were resolved as happily and easily as that one. Because of the cooperation of the young people, the problems were not centered inside the building, but outside in the parking lot. Ultimately we had to deal with smoking, alcohol, drugs, pornography, sex and guns before we were through.

The choir director at the Post Chapel was the post Provost Marshall. I mentioned to him that the parking lot was a major concern. "It is hard enough for me to keep tabs on what's going on with 50 or 60 youngsters inside the building, but I need help concerning what's going on outside."

The cooperation of the Military Police in patrolling the parking lot was exemplary. They checked vehicles, personnel who didn't belong there, anything that looked suspicious. It was a sad disappointment to learn that the supplier of most of the pornographic material was the father of two of the finest youngsters in the club. I never would have suspected it from knowing his children.

I never did learn who was supplying the marijuana, alcohol and guns. I was busy working inside with the youngsters. They always tipped me off when something improper was expected and I kept the Provost Marshall informed. The young people themselves were beautiful. It was always an adult influence that was the basis of any problem.

There were a few events in connection with the club that are worth describing.

Because of some of the funerals and funeral arrangements I'd had to perform, I'd become friends with the undertaker from a nearby city. The club decided to have a Halloween party complete with Spook Alley. I asked him if we could borrow a coffin. He explained that it would be illegal for anyone to get into a coffin before its final occupant was placed in it. He would not be permitted to sell it if someone had tried it out. "However, I have a cheap wooden coffin that is supposed to be used for cremation. You can have it." With his help, the help of the club members and several young enlisted men, we set up our Spook Alley. We placed the coffin in a separate small room through which the costumed club members would have to pass before entering the main ball room.

One of the LDS enlisted men, Lloyd Hawkes, climbed into the coffin. We coated his face with white flour. He held a flashlight with blue cellophane over it in his hands. When he turned on the light, his face looked ghastly blue-white with a pock-marked disintegrating appearance. We sprinkled embalming fluid around the semi-darkened room to give it the appropriate odor. We added flowers and somber music for atmosphere.

The young girls all screamed and panicked at the right times . . . especially if the corpse chose to sit up suddenly, which it frequently did.

The Undertaker promised to have a Gypsy Fortune Teller come and set up a tent in the corner of the ball room. She was the hit of the evening.

One of the young ladies came to me bubbling with excitement. "She told me I was going to have a fight with my boyfriend, and I did. And that I was going to find someone new, and I did. Then I'd decide I liked my old boyfriend better, so I'd make up with him. And I did. Now I have to go back and get another reading to see what else is going to happen!"

I scratched my head. "How long since your last reading?"

"About twenty minutes."

"All that happened in that short a time?"

"Yes. Isn't it wonderful!" And off she rushed to have the rest of her life planned by the Gypsy.

It made me happy to see young people concerned with problems of this kind rather than the ones I'd seen other young people struggling with in Korea. I thought to myself, this is the way childhood should be.

Chapter 34.

The Inter-Faith Sunday School / Ministerial Association

The Post had an inter-disciplinary Protestant Sunday School. Chaplain White learned that I had once been a Sunday School teacher, so he decided to put me in charge of it. The Sunday School had over 350 children who attended it, plus several adult classes. We had from 20 to 30 people in each class. They were taught in four different locations throughout the post. That meant I had to oversee a staff of about twenty volunteer teachers. These teachers represented most of the major Protestant churches. Their backgrounds were varied. It was gratifying to see them setting aside their differences and working together, and enjoying teaching the children.

I do not recall that any major problems arose. Most of the complications came in the form of assigning and juggling classrooms, seeing to it that every teacher had a copy of the correct lesson manual, and that the Sunday School library was well stocked with visual aids, chalk and erasers, etc.

One constant concern was finding substitute teachers when someone was away for the weekend or on maneuvers, or whatever.

Chaplain White's office did most of the administrational duties, so I worked very closely with his Assistants regarding it.

I also did a lot of teacher training so we had a pool of regular and substitute teachers available.

Between my regular Chapel Services, choir practices, the Teen-Age Club, the Post Sunday School, my character guidance lectures, administrative duties for my assigned unit, other surrounding units and hospital duties, I was kept very busy. In addition, when the weather warmed up in the spring we began to hold Vesper Services one night a week. They were usually about forty five minutes long. They consisted of singing several hymns and an appropriate thought for the day.

Outside of the Post there is a hill that has a cross about twenty feet tall on the top of it. The cross has lights mounted on the front of it. When viewed from the back the lights themselves don't show, just the glow from them. When a group of worshipers are seated in the benches facing the back of the cross, the cross appears to be glowing against the Arizona sunset, a soft warm breeze is blowing, and you are singing God's praises, it never fails to be a magic moment. You realize how grateful you are to your Creator for all the beauty He has placed on this earth. You feel thankful you live in a land where you can worship Him for all He has done.

Chaplain White was approached by the Ministerial Association in Bisbee, Arizona to have a representative from the Post join its membership. He appointed me. That was one of the first times, to my knowledge, that a Mormon served as a member of a Ministerial Association. It was a good experience that led to greater understanding and cooperation among the various faiths.

Chapter 35.

Proper Disciplinary Measures

Sometimes the job of Chaplain puts you squarely in the middle of a controversy. How do you resolve divergent viewpoints and still remain friends with everybody? Sometimes you can't.

One afternoon I had a stream of unhappy men come through my office with the same complaint. Three or four men in their barracks had not kept their quarters clean and tidy enough to pass inspection. The Major had restricted the whole unit to quarters for the weekend. Most of the men had plans for the weekend and were very unhappy about the restriction. It was clearly a form of mass punishment, and amounted to improper protocol. I called the Major, informed him that I had had numerous complaints, and asked him respectfully to reconsider.

"Chaplain, I've had trouble getting those guys to clean up their quarters for a month now. I'm tired of looking the other way. I figure if I restrict everybody, the peer pressure will get hot enough to get them to do the job."

"I understand what you're trying to do, sir, but instead of getting the offenders to clean up their act, it's making everyone resentful. Couldn't you restrict just the offenders, sir?

"I've tried it. It didn't work."

"I'm sorry, sir, but this isn't working either."

"Chappie, just mind your own business and let me take care of mine. Okay?"

"Sorry, sir. This is my business. It's not fair to restrict everybody because of a few."

"Damn it, Chappie, butt out!"

"Sorry, sir, but if I can't get you to change your mind, I'll have to go to the Colonel about it."

"You can go to . . . anyplace you choose, Chappie! The decision stands!"

I walked across the street from my chapel to the Group Headquarters building. I asked to see the Colonel. He was a well-respected older gentleman that I had only talked to a couple of times before. His Adjutant ushered me into his office. He greeted me warmly.

"Chaplain, it's nice to see you. How's everything going?" I took his question literally. "Sir, I have a problem. Several men have complained to me that their Battalion has been restricted to quarters for the weekend because a few men chronically have failed to pass inspection. It looks like mass punishment. I can understand what the Major is trying to do, to bring about peer pressure, but there must be a better way."

"Have you talked to the Major about it?"

"Yes, sir. I told him if he wouldn't change his mind I intended to inform you about it. He gave me permission to come here."

"Chaplain, you don't ever need anyone's permission to see me about anything. Thank you for letting me know." He called his Executive Officer into the office. "Did you hear what's happening?" The Exec answered "Yes, sir."

"Take care of it."

I spent the next twenty minutes in small talk with the Colonel while I could overhear the Executive officer on the telephone in the next office literally turning the air blue as he gave the Major direct orders to reverse himself.

After that I was popular with the men, but the Major didn't like me. Later we had a chance to talk about it. He felt I had betrayed him by going behind his back to the Colonel. I reminded him I had talked to him first and only went to the Colonel after warning him I would. He remembered that was true, but it didn't change his feelings towards me.

On another occasion some men came by to tell me that their buddy, a private, was being picked on by their Sergeant. I decided to investigate and find out what was really going on. I started with the Sergeant.

"Chaplain, that kid is a screw-up. I've had it with him. He breaks all the rules. I can't let him get away with it or I'll lose all hope of maintaining discipline throughout the whole unit."

I had to agree with him, basically. But on the other hand I felt he tended to go a little too far in perpetually handing out the most unpleasant duties to this particular soldier. "I'll talk to him and see why he keeps causing problems. If we can't resolve it, maybe we can get him transferred to another unit." I then talked to the private.

He felt it was a life-and-death struggle between him and the Sergeant and he "would rather die than give in."

"Give in to what? What do you hope to gain? I don't understand all this hostility. Explain it to me."

"See, you're on his side. I can see it. Otherwise why all the questions!"

"Your friends asked me to. They're concerned about you. I'm here because of them."

Gradually he began talking and letting his feelings out. "The Sarge's had it in for me since the first day I got here." He went on explaining at length. There were a lot of little things that had gone wrong until he felt overwhelmed.

I asked him, "If I can get the Sarge to back off, will you work with me and quit doing things that irritate him and cause problems for yourself?" I realized that he knew better than to do many of the things he did. He was deliberately causing problems. The Sergeant knew some of them were deliberate, but he was underestimating this soldier's capabilities in general.

Next I went back to the Sarge and asked for his cooperation. His attitude was "I'll break that little punk's spirit. He'll conform, or else! When he starts to show me he's shaping up, then I'll start backing off. Not before."

"Sarge, I want you to let up first. It's up to you to take the first step. You're his superior. You're more experienced. Actually, you're in control. He's so emotionally involved he can't take the first step."

"Never happen, Chaplain. He's got to do it. It's not my position to make the change."

"Okay. If that's the way you want it . . . but keep this in mind, I'll be at your elbow until you change your mind." With that I chose to stay in close proximity to the Sergeant for the rest of the day. He had to curtail his usually distasteful language. It made him uncomfortable to have to watch every word.

Unknown to him, the next morning I was standing close behind him as he conducted his regular company formation. He was swearing as usual. I put my hands over my ears. The men were snickering in ranks. This upset the Sergeant. He turned around and saw me. "How long have you been there?" he asked in surprise.

"Too long" was my reply. He knew what I meant.

I spent a large part of the morning just hanging around him, talking to the men, asking pointless questions, making small talk. Finally the Sergeant asked, "Don't you have something to do, sir?"

"Nope. I've decided to just enjoy your company."

"But you're interfering with my work. I can't concentrate with you looking over my shoulder."

"My schedule's pretty much my own. I've been very careful not to interfere with your duties. I'm only here to help. What more could you ask?"

"I know why you're here."

"I'm sure you do. And I intend to stay just as long as you need me."

"Okay, Chaplain. I get the picture. I'll take the first step. But I expect you to follow up with him so he fulfills his end of the bargain."

"You know I will. Thanks, Sarge." With that I left and he looked relieved.

That night at the Mess Hall his Captain came over to me. "I understand you're spending a lot of time with my Sergeant. Is there a problem?"

"Oh, no, sir. We're just good friends."

"That's not the way I heard it. If there's a problem with one of my men, I want to know about it."

"If I felt you needed to be involved, sir, I would have come to you. Whenever something can be settled with fewer people to complicate matters, that's the way I prefer to work. Your Sergeant is a very capable man. He's handling everything. If you wish, I'll keep you informed, but I don't see anything for you to do at present, sir."

"Well, I heard you attended our company formation this morning."

"I apologize for that. His language was a bit colorful."

The Captain started to laugh. "I would have liked to have seen his face when he turned around and saw you standing there holding your ears."

"It did make a point, sir."

As I started to leave the mess hall I saw Captain Glover from my old Headquarters Company in Korea sitting there. He got up and came over to me with his hand extended. "I promoted your boy."

"How've you been? When did you get here?"

"Yesterday."

"How are things with the unit in Korea?"

"Well, we finished the business in Pusan, so everything was rather slow. Then I finished my tour, so here I am. Why didn't you tell me Wixom was the best crane operator in the battalion?"

"I did."

"Yeah, but you didn't make me believe it. When the new Chaplain arrived he chose an assistant from his own church, Methodist. So I assigned Wixom to drive the jeep for somebody else. He asked me if he could work on the heavy equipment instead. We had plenty of other jeep drivers, so I decided to go along. He was the best I had. No nonsense. Never drunk or late. Kept his mouth shut and did his job."

"I told you I always chose the best."

"Next time I'll listen."

Another pleasant surprise awaited me. The young LDS soldier I had befriended at the Lompoc Disciplinary Barracks, the one who was incarcerated for murder, was now released and stationed at Fort Huachuca. He had read the Book of Mormon, received an answer to his prayers, and been ordained an Elder. His life was turned around. It was a joy to see what repentance and a testimony can do.

Chapter 36.

My Technique for Dealing with Problems

Sometimes individual soldiers have overwhelming problems to deal with. Illness or death in their families back home, inter-denominational marriage plans, whatever. The Chaplain's job is to sit, listen, help sort it all out and find solutions. Usually the solution becomes clear once the problem is defined. I found that non-directive counseling techniques worked best for me in clarifying problems. After all, the person directly involved would know a lot more about the situation than I would. I just helped by providing the perspective of distance and acting like a mirror to reflect his thoughts.

If the problem were one that could be resolved through army channels, it was one of the simpler ones. For example, the allotment checks for the family of one of the men were not being sent. The solution required that certain forms be filled out and forwarded to the appropriate payroll department. As a rule I made it my practice not to go through channels in the way most people did. That is, I did not approach the Commander of the unit that was responsible for the paper work and ask him to assign it down through channels to the clerk who ultimately typed the forms. I worked in the opposite direction.

I went to the clerk and asked what forms were needed in order to accomplish what it was I wanted to do. This made him feel important. He'd bring out the forms. I'd type them with his assistance/instruction.

Once they were accurately completed, I'd hand carry them up through channels for the necessary signatures of approval. This cut the time to less than half for getting the job done. The request went only up through channels, not down through them then back up again.

Also it provided the commanding officer with ready-made solutions that required only his signature instead of making him determine what was needed, then assigning it out, then checking to see if it was done properly.

As a result of this policy, when I completed my tour of duty at Fort Huachuca, a farewell party was given in my honor. At that party one of the enlisted men from the personnel office said, "This is the only guy on this post who got everything he asked for out of this office." It was meant as a compliment to me. It also revealed quite a bit about how that office operated.

Chapter 37.

Personal Matters

I was kept very busy. Marguerite had a limited social life, yet she managed to keep her time well filled. We decided that we should buy a new car. After all, the blue Plymouth had 50,000 miles on it. By today's standards that isn't much, but we were young.

We found a sporty two tone tomato-red and white Plymouth with spoke wheels in Bisbee that we just had to have! It became widely recognizable all over the Post. One day the MPs pulled her over. They apologized. "We thought it was the Chaplain in his pink cloud. We just wanted to say hello." I had done a lot of work with the MPs, so it was merely a social contact. From that time forth we called that car "the Pink Cloud."

The father of two of the outstanding children of the Teen-Age Club was the third highest ranking officer on the Post. His wife was one of the nicest, most wholesome down-to-earth ladies I've ever met. She went out of her way to become friends with Marguerite. She gave a baby shower for her which was attended by almost all of the officers' wives from the General on down. It was an exciting time in our lives.

Our son was born in late January. I don't remember much about that day except I had to give two Character Guidance lectures and hold a choir practice in addition to checking at the hospital. My Assistants later told me I was a basket case I was so disorganized.

I went to the hospital in the morning and afternoon to see my wife. She was asleep. I left her red roses and a box of chocolates. I went back that evening after ducking out of choir practice. It was wonderful for the three of us to share those moments.

We named our son Stephen. Stevie changed our lives. He didn't want to sleep at night. We had to guard him constantly from Butch's affectionate advances. Those were happy and fulfilling times.

Section V :

Summary

Chapter 38.

Looking Back

My mission was one of the highlights of my life. I can say the same about my military career as a Chaplain. In looking back, I wish to summarize what it involved. Here are a few of the high spots.

I performed my first marriage while stationed at Camp Cooke, California. I performed funerals and graveside services. One of the saddest was for the one year-old baby of a young couple at Fort Huachuca just a short time after our own son was born.

I preached sermons and held joint services with Chaplains from all the major Protestant churches: Baptist, Christian Scientist, Church of the Nazarene, Disciples of Christ, Episcopalian, Lutheran, Methodist, Presbyterian, etc. I came to appreciate their faith and sincerity.

Today when someone raises the question "Are Mormons Christians?" I wonder at their common sense. As a Chaplain representing the Church of Jesus Christ of Latter-day Saints I held joint services with all the Chaplains mentioned above. I gave sermons, lead in the prayers, scripture readings, and recitations, conducted the singing, performed the marriages, funerals, etc. Not one of those chaplains or congregations ever once questioned my Christianity. If the ordained leaders from all the Protestant churches accept the idea that Mormons are Christians, why do some of their lay members have any confusion regarding that fact?

In addition to the Protestant ministers I served with, I shared the chapel at Fort Huachuca with two Catholic priests whose lengthy philosophical discussions increased my understanding and appreciation for their devotion to the Lord . . . and theirs of mine. I shared discussions with numerous Jewish Rabbis as well.

I was an officer in the military who worked on a personal level with everyone regardless of rank. The confidences of generals, privates, and everyone in between were shared with me. I treasured and protected those confidences.

I observed men undergoing the most trying of circumstances, in foxholes under fire, newly wounded in the M.A.S.H., undergoing lengthy recovery treatments in army hospitals stateside, in prison, in emotional pain over unfaithful mates, experiencing the joy of feeding the hungry and dressing the poor and needy, in doubt over the possibility of being ordered to face death themselves or having the responsibility for ordering others to face it, in remorse and repentance over indiscretions, in joy from finding solace in God's plan . . . Our Heavenly Father has given us a wonderful plan. It is exciting. It is varied. It is challenging. It is never dull or boring. It is life!

Life makes a lot more sense when we can put everything into the context of His wonderful plan. That was the joy of the chaplain's work . . . reminding my brothers and sisters in the military that we are all here on earth to enjoy our Creator's plan, and that we should view every situation that arises in that context.

I was involved in the lives of my fellow men in positive ways. That was the common link between being a missionary and being a chaplain.

In the month of May I received my Honorable Discharge. What did the future hold? I was a married man with a family. I had no job. No specific goals. What should I do next?

Well, that's another story.